SUCCESSFUL RETAILING

SUCCESSFUL RETAILING

Your Step-by-Step Guide
to Avoiding Pitfalls and Finding Profit
as an Independent Retailer

Second Edition

Paula Wardell

UPSTART PUBLISHING COMPANY, INC.
The Small Business Publishing Company
Dover, New Hampshire

Published by Upstart Publishing Company, Inc.
A Division of Dearborn Publishing Group, Inc.
12 Portland Street
Dover, New Hampshire 03820
(800) 235-8866 or (603) 749-5071

Library of Congress Cataloging-in-Publication Data
Wardell, Paula.
     Successful retailing: your step-by-step guide to avoiding pitfalls and finding profit as an independent retailer/Paula Wardell. — 2nd ed.
     p.   cm.
     Includes index.
     ISBN 0-936894-56-3
     1. Retail trade—Management. I. Title.
     HF5429.W335 1993
     658.8'7—dc20   93-9082
                                               CIP

Cover design by Kozman Graphics, Portsmouth, NH.

Printed in the United States of America
10 9 8 7 6 5 4 3 2 1

For a complete catalog of Upstart's small business publications, call (800) 235-8866.

Table of Contents

Introduction

There are many dimensions to the art of merchandising. Each dimension has facets like a cut gem. Imagine that each gem is cut and polished to make it shine, sparkle, fascinate and entrance you. These gems then interlock to become one large, incredible jewel. Any one out-of-place or flawed component affects the whole. Your store is that magnificent jewel. For your store to shine, every component must work individually and in harmony with the others. Merchandising and inventory management create that gem, and your actions generate the sparkle.

Many retailers have gone into retail cash rich and information poor. This book addresses this problem to better your chances in retail. I want to see people achieving their dreams. The information in this book prepares you to maneuver around, over, under or through the obstacles that come at you in inventory management. With the high dollar amount you have invested in inventory, you need all the tools the big stores use.

First-time owners will benefit from going through all sections of this book before tackling the formulas. Practicing after such an overview reinforces the flow of inventory control principles. Existing store owners may skip to chapters that answer your current questions. The handbook progresses to build on the knowledge from previous chapters, so sequential reading provides additional benefits. For example, say you want to buy your opening inventory. You need to understand several aspects to complement your good taste and well-written store concept. You need answers to questions such as:

- What are your sales projections for the total store? For each month?
- What departments and subclasses are there in the store?
- What are the sales projections and inventory levels for each class? For each month?
- What is the OTB (open to buy)? For the store and for each department?
- What markdowns are anticipated?

These questions can be answered when you also know:

- what time of year you will be opening your new store;

- what market research information tells you about your target market; and
- other environmental factors.

You need time and market research to help you answer these and additional questions. Analyzing departments and subclasses and other information further refines your ability to answer these questions with confidence. We all say we don't have enough time, yet not taking the necessary time to plan can cost you money. Before you say how much inventory you will carry, you will want to project sales projections, as well as the stockturn. Then you will start hacking away at figuring Open to Buy. The first two chapters address these valuable planning and evaluating tools. They create the groundwork for your total store planning needs. A lot of math appears, but the formulas are simple. We'll define terms in the merchandising OTB (Open to Buy) plan.

Stockturn

BOM —Beginning of the Month Inventory

EOM—End of the Month Inventory

S/S Ratio—Stock to Sales Ratio

Average Markon

Cumulative Markon

Markdowns

Shrinkage

Retail Markon

Vendors

Purchase Orders

Other terms and details that relate to the total process such as shipping terms, dating terms and so on will also be covered. Many help you negotiate better, cut costs or make better use of your money.

Looking at a classical organization chart of a retail operation, you would see a hierarchy of job titles that indicate the job description of each. As an independent retail owner you wear the hats of president, treasurer, vice president and general merchandise manager, personnel manager, credit and office manager, ad manager, merchandise manager(s), buyer(s) and salesperson(s). While we're concentrating on merchandising and inventory management in this book, this information and control affects many decisions if you are the owner; that is everything from financial officer to salesperson to buyer.

When we concentrate on buying functions, you will see immediately why larger stores have people who solely:

1. shop and research the market for new trends, items, new resources;

2. develop a merchandising strategy in relation to the target markets, trends, resources, price points, and so on;

3. control stock levels in relation to planned goals of sales, mark downs, markon, turn and gross profit;

4. analyze merchandising information from reports on everything from sales and stock performance to vendor analysis to the departmental operating statement;

5. negotiate terms from vendors, discounts and programs in areas of growth;

6. impart information to department heads and sales staff;

7. identify and take advantage of fast-selling items, also take appropriate action when slow sellers are spotted;

8. maintain balanced stocks in each store (when you grow) and keep the appropriate assortments;

9. stay on top of open orders and correct mis-shipments due to no orders or early delivery;

10. shop the competition;

11. consider and recommend physical improvements that aid achieving merchandising objectives.

Welcome to retailing! Few industries are more exciting. When you have more than one store you, as a buyer, will visit those stores to observe the stock levels and glean information from department managers and the sales staff. This list hasn't touched on your responsibilities to:

- define the merchandise presentation and work with visual display personnel
- work with the ad department
- develop and train staff
- work with the warehouse and distribution personnel
- control shortage.

Finally, congratulations on your promotion—to janitor!

Examples of the merchandising formulas and forms are filled out within the chapters in which the methods are explained. Blank forms for you to photocopy for your own use are in Appendix III (see p. 139).

The first chapter contains a lot of math used in buying and planning. The purchase order is discussed in Chapter 2 because of the importance of that one form to your whole business. Capturing the data and utilizing the formulas for management purposes is covered in the third chapter, Inventory Management. Chapter 4 addresses the financial aspects of your business and how they tie into inventory control.

The balance of the book attacks the nuts and bolts of decision-making through Merchandising Techniques, Chapter 5, and Buying Strategies, Chapter 6.

These areas are ongoing operational and buying processes in retail. Situations that I have seen in my years as a consultant to small, independent retailers have been cited throughout the book as examples. Good luck! Please take note of special services and notes in the back of the book.

Thank you for doing business with me!

Chapter 1

Open To Buy: The Merchandise Plan

WHY DO FORMAL OTB PLANNING?

The majority of retail owners of small independent stores have not had retail experience. Sometimes they have sold for a department store or even managed a location of a chain. As an owner, you wear many hats. This proves, most of the time, to be an overwhelming experience. Store owners ask me why they should plan their inventory as I suggest. After they learn the ins and outs of OTB (Open To Buy) planning, they more fully understand the reasons I am about to cite to you.

Professional buying practices and inventory control will help:

- Control your overall cash flow for the operation;
- Reduce your markdowns, thus increasing gross profit;
- Control interest costs on borrowed funds, creating better cash management;
- Improve your company's productivity; and
- Strengthen your store's image, thus your position in the marketplace.

These points are important to every store's existence. Consider the following, which further stresses the need to keep a close rein on your inventory, purchase plans and inventory management techniques: The inventory purchases figure of the "Cost of Goods Sold" on the Profit and Loss statement may go as high as 75 percent of gross sales. On the balance sheet, 50 percent to 70 percent of your assets is in inventory. What an asset! If 55 to 75 percent of every dollar is for direct purchases, any business novice would consider you deeply disturbed if you didn't work with a concise method to track and control those percentages.

Our goals in merchandise planning are:

- Maintain an inventory neither too large nor too small for projected customer demand.
- Time delivery of purchases so that merchandise is available for sale when sales are anticipated, not earlier or later.
- Keep purchases in line with the store's ability to pay for them.
- Have funds available to purchase new goods as needed.

1

The limited capital of the independent retailer makes merchandise planning vital. Overall, the merchandise plan provides the guide for the buyer/owner in the attempt to secure the desired level of sales. Remember, inventory supports sales. To do so efficiently and profitably, you must plan inventory levels and purchases for control, and obtain the facts needed to make decisions to ensure that control. This efficiency is highly desirable as opposed to reacting continually to some level of crisis.

We will be using the **Retail Inventory Method** of accounting. This is the accounting system in which all transactions affecting inventory—sales, purchases, markdowns, transfers, returns-to-vendor—are recorded at the retail price. As an owner/buyer, it is important to have these figures organized and readily accessible. This will constitute your Inventory Control and Management.

Formal merchandise planning solves the problem of how to organize the figures. I have spent much time with clients digging out past figures from financial statements and pieces of paper filed away and hardly glanced at. These people were generally having lots of problems, too.

The difference between large stores and independent retailers starts in the organizational formatting of the figures and the source of the planning. The accounting department provides merchandising and buying staff with last year figures, as well as operation figures for each department on a form. Even after buyers put their own projections together, these go back to upper management in the merchandising and financial control levels for approval and revision.

The single store owner does not get this "luxury." (Though I don't know of any department store or chain store buyer who would call this a luxury!). You conduct all of the input and review it yourself. This is a good reason to get input from sales staff and customers about merchandise. Their likes and dislikes help balance out some of your own thoughts when planning.

Define what business you are in. Do this by knowing your target market. Staying focused and making decisions that relate to the objectives of your business prevent you from being sidetracked. I have witnessed retailers who lost sight of their original concept and the customer they targeted. They confused everyone, even themselves, by buying all sorts of merchandise. The focus was lost and so was the customer.

This lack of focus and commitment to the store's concept results in lost dollars spent on inventory, marketing, and more. It could even mean closing the doors permanently. You have all experienced the feeling of confusion when you've walked into a store that just didn't seem to "know who it was." Unrelated merchandise assaulted your senses. You walked out—a lost customer, probably forever.

GETTING STARTED

Write down your business definition in terms of:

- Target market
- Price range
- Customer service
- Competition
- Sales method
- Range of vendors
- Overall objectives

If you write a formal business plan, these sections will be well covered. A couple of paragraphs suffice for daily guidance purposes. Just do it! And refer to it daily.

The tracking and control methods are the guts of this book.

Your store may need 50 to 70 percent of your total current assets in inventory. If it isn't timely, in the right proportion, or is made up of the wrong mix, well, I have seen the remnants and the difficult road to recovery—if that was feasible for the store. Money not tied up in inventory might be better used toward new equipment, better and more training, signage, new or increased coverage of promotions or additional sales staff, all of which might generate higher sales for the store. The opposite scenario of not having enough inventory in the proper departments causes lost sales and customers.

You get the idea and my point. Now on to work and increased profits.

UNDERSTANDING AND FINDING TARGET MARKETS

Key to the development and continuation of your store is knowing your market. Everyone talks about your "target market." Just what exactly is that? Very simply, a group of people with a set of common characteristics. Based on the set of characteristics, it follows that the buying habits, needs and such will be similar. That is why you hear business people refer to target marketing.

No store has just one target market. There is overlap of various target markets. However, you will have a primary target market. When you first envisioned your store concept you most likely saw a need you wanted your store's inventory to fill. Understanding this target group of the population aids you in setting sales objectives, pricing structure and other aspects of your store. Their characteristics indicate wants and/or needs. These translate into store concepts, services and products to fill the wants and needs.

How do you know what this target market is? Research. You must spend some time in the library to learn about the trends in the industry you are interested in. If you come from that industry, you have very likely armed yourself with that information because you read your trade papers and other related publications. Many databases in the library provide a wealth of information on any subject you could imagine. InfoTrac is one such database of published magazine articles. Other databases may cover newspapers or trade journals.

This is secondary research since the information has been published. There is also primary research, where you go directly to the potential consumer. Most of us have been stopped in a mall or other location to answer a few questions. More extensive primary research would include focus groups of people from broad or select groups, depending on the purpose of the research.

There are sources to learn about who you want (and need) to target. The very basic information you are looking for includes the range in income and age, work attributes (two-income household; blue- or white-collar), sex, education, household composition and where they live. Is this group (read target market) growing in numbers? Do they have some kind of specific needs such as can be seen in the aging population or the mini baby-boom? Understand that this type of information will aid your site selection process as well for opening a new store or moving an existing one. You want to locate where your target market is willing to shop for your type of product.

This information is readily available in Census Bureau reports, Department of Commerce reports, data collection by business groups such as Economic Development Councils in a city or area. The Survey of Buying Power is published bi-annually by *Sales and Marketing Management* magazine. The July issue presents population by age group, households, retail sales for six categories and "Effective Buying Income." The October issue includes total retail sales for seven lines of merchandise, population projections and retail sales projections. Look for national trends in your target market and then find the target market locally. Local statistics can come from Census Bureau and other agencies as well as surveys by local publications.

Here are some examples of information on target markets and the source of the information.

"Treating Kids as Customers," an article in *Stores* magazine (published by the National Retail Federation) about the offspring of baby boomers as a market gives statistics on age, average weekly income, expenditures and savings of 4- to 12-year-olds.

"Recent Survey Shows Today's Children Have Deep Pockets," an article in *Publishers Weekly,* shows the dollar and percentage increase in income, spending and savings for the same group of the population. This article also has a graph of the percentage of children ages 4 to 12 making independent trips to stores. As a business owner, this means this target market is spending their own money based on their own decision-making process. You must ask your-self (and research) what they are purchasing. What do they want to purchase if they could find it?

"As U.S. consumers age, so will products and pitches," an article in the *Kansas City Star* includes statistics on the 50-plus population. It stated that this target market owns 77 percent of all the financial assets in America; owns 80 percent of all the money in U.S. savings and loan institutions; purchases 43 percent of all new domestic cars and 48 percent of all luxury cars; spends more money on travel and recreation than any other age group. What kind of shopping experience would you come up with knowing this information? Where are they living? Moving to? Visiting?

The *American Demographics* magazine is just that, a wealth of information about population trends. Trade associations may also have information on consumers that buy the products you want to sell as well as other information about stores. Since associations are usually national (sometimes international) in scope, you will learn what others are doing in other cities. Check the *Encyclopedia of Associations* (in the library reference section, of course) for the associations that pertain to your product.

If market research is new to you, don't worry. Throw yourself on the mercy of the reference librarian. It's their job and they love to do it, so leave your guilt at home when you go to the library. Also, pick up a copy of *Finding Facts Fast* by Alden Todd. He'll make you a pro at finding meaningful information.

PLANNING TERMS AND BASICS

Your store exists to provide a service to consumers. Wait! You say, I sell mer-chandise. Yes, you do and the fact that you make available certain products the consumer wants and/or needs, then he or she has access to them. Remember, it takes a certain inventory level to support a certain sales level at any specific time.

Your target market needs a selection to choose from, has different motivations to purchase at various times of the year, and various sources to choose from. Very few stores have a captured audience for long, if ever. This supports the idea of service.

Always knowing your concept and reason for being is your guiding light through many decisions in inventory management.

Generally, **Inventory Control**, comprised of tracking systems, ensures that sufficient inventory is on hand or on order. **Inventory Management** includes those systems and record-keeping that provide objective data upon which to base decisions on when to buy and how, what to stock, vendor analysis and the financial control of the business's inventory.

We will first look at the merchandise or Open To Buy plan that is part of Inventory Control. Actually, retailing goes through these phases continually:

- Plan Open To Buy
- Track sales, purchases, mark-downs and such
- Evaluate sales figures and all other components
- Evaluate plans and revise plans
- Create new plans for new trends and changes in the inventory movement

Some of these steps occur simultaneously depending on the systems you set up. The nature of retail creates a chain of events and simultaneous actions. There exists a constant flow of goods through the store selling and restocking (some reorders and some new stock). **This flow depends on your systems.**

You can see the difficulty in defining Inventory Control and Inventory Management. In this handbook, we will work with the Open To Buy plan, the basis for all the phases, first. This is the math and inventory control portion of merchandising. The Open To Buy encompasses all of the mathematical tactics to control your inventory. **The resulting dollar figure of Open To Buy will be the control figure you'll work with continually, no matter what phase of store management you're conducting.** The other phases will be discussed in full detail in Inventory Management and Financial Control. Then we'll build up to more sophisticated aspects of decision making in Merchandising Techniques and Buying Strategies.

The language of any industry can seem foreign at first. Review these terms, here, to assist you through learning to construct an Open To Buy plan more easily.

MERCHANDISE PLANNING AND OPEN TO BUY TERMS

Stockturn: The number of times the average inventory totally turns through the store (sold and replaced), usually examined on an annual basis.

Stock To Sales Ratio: The relationship between retail sales and the amount of inventory, planned or actual, at the beginning of the month at retail.

Open To Buy (OTB): The dollar amount of inventory to be received in any month needed to bring inventory to the level planned for the next month.

Safety Levels: Planned levels of inventory for an item. This takes into account the lead time for the receipt of goods to prevent out-of-stock situations.

Markon: The percentage amount of the retail price on an item over and above cost. This figure is always in relationship to the retail price. In this light then the markon is the difference between retail and cost.

Average Markon: Markon averaged between several items being considered for purchase, usually for a promotion.

Department: The overall classification of similar types of goods, such as dresses, nonalcoholic beverages, linens, etc.

Classification and Subclassification: Some stores break down the departments further. For small stores, it is best to use departments and subclasses. For example, the subclasses for dresses would be—evening, prom, business, sleeveless, summer and so on.

Percentage Increase <Decrease>: the percentage increase or decrease of sales in a period of time, say a month, over the same period in the previous year. You will evaluate increases and decreases in your departments and your total store.

Cumulative Markon: The markon attained over a period of time. Just as in initial markon, this is the difference between total cost and total retail of all goods.

Shrinkage: That amount of inventory that reduces your inventory figure due to a loss either on paper or the actual loss from the store.

Beginning Of The Month (BOM): The inventory level in terms of retail dollars needed at the beginning of the month.

End Of The Month (EOM): The amount of inventory in terms of retail dollars left after sales and markdowns from the BOM.

Markdowns: The dollar amount reducing the retail price of your inventory.

Merchandise Manager: The person over the buyers for a department or departments in a large retail operation.

Divisional Merchandise Manager: The person over the Merchandise Managers.

MARKON AND PRICING

It is vital to understand price and markon before we go on. First, price.

For all practicality, there are three retail prices:

1. The original retail price.
2. The current price (more or less than the original).
3. The retail selling price—when the sale is actually made.

In our planning of inventory, we will take into consideration mark-downs that take the price of an item down from the original to a new current price. This affects the overall retail value of your inventory. Profitability is affected by markdowns, thus if ignored with other planning techniques, the business ends up in a cash crunch quickly.

Let's embark into the following calculations of markon. **Remember: All merchandise planning in dollars is done at the retail level, not cost.** Set your thinking to relate, always, to retail.

Planning Markon

The difference between the retail price and the cost price (what you paid the manufacturer for the item) **relates to the retail price**, not the cost price. Some display and examples are in order now.

Percentage of retail markon calculation:

$$\frac{\$ \text{ RETAIL} - \$ \text{ COST}}{\$ \text{ RETAIL}} = \text{MARKON percent}$$

OK you say, but I don't know the retail price yet. I just bought the merchandise and need to put a retail price on the item.

Let's say a 50 percent markon is standard for your type of store. Markon relates to retail, so the difference between 100 percent (the retail price is the 100 percent value of the item at initial markon) and the markon percentage gives you the related figure for the formula to figure the retail price. You know the cost price, you know the retail markon, so the complement of markon relates to cost. Let's look at this in an example:

$$\frac{\$ \text{ COST}}{100\% - \text{MARKON }\%} = \$ \text{ RETAIL}$$

If the cost of an item is \$10.00 and the retail markon is 50 percent, then the retail price is:

$$\frac{\$ 10.00}{100\% - 50\%} = \$ \text{ RETAIL}$$

or $$\frac{\$ 10.00}{.50} = \$ 20.00$$

Let's jog the high school algebra memories here a bit. You can't divide by a percentage, so get rid of it by dividing by 100 (you do the reverse when you are figuring percentage increases). Play with this on your calculator through two more examples:

$$\text{Cost} = \$14.90$$

Markon for your store = 45%

$$\frac{\$14.90}{100\% - 45\%} = \frac{\$14.90}{.55} = \$27.09$$

One more:

$$Cost = \$74.50$$

Markon for your store = 52%

$$\frac{\$74.5}{100\% - 52\%} = \frac{\$74.5}{.48} = \$155.20$$

Always remember, the retail price is the 100 percent value of the item you are working with just as net sales is the 100 percent marker for the Profit and Loss Statement. You can buy a profit wheel at a stationery store that will figure the retail for you by lining up a percentage markon with the cost amount. It will serve you well, though, to master this simple calculation. Let's look at a situation where you can utilize the formula previously presented.

Checking a Competitor's Markon

To evaluate a competitor's markon, look for an item that you both carry (or one that you looked at but passed up buying). When you know the retail and the cost, you can work the first version of the retail markon formula that was illustrated.

Example: Tootsie's Toddlers Shop is one of your children shop's competitors and they are carrying the corduroy overalls you passed up.

The retail = $48.00

The cost = $23.00 (your notes from market have provided you with this information)

So, you use the formula:

$$\frac{\$\,RETAIL - \$\,COST}{\$\,RETAIL} = MARKON\ \%$$

And plug in the values:

$$\frac{\$48.00 - \$23.00}{\$48.00} = 52.08\%$$

You now know that your competitor's markon is 52 percent, and you can compare it with your own. There may be other items you check in the same manner with this and other competitors.

Goal in Planning Markon

To attain a markon that will cover probable expenses, profit goal, probable reductions, and miscellaneous costs (like alterations).

Obviously, you won't deviate (greatly) from industry standards. Appropriate exceptions will be covered in Chapter 6, Buying Strategies. If your market uses a 50 percent markon traditionally, you may evaluate specific items for additional markon, but not all of your stock. You may even take a shorter markon to push an item through the store faster or on a basic item your customers buy continually.

PLANNING MARKDOWNS

Look at your historical figures or, if a new store, check industry standards. This may not be readily accessible information. Remember that certain months in the year will have a heavier percentage of markdowns than others. Consider, also, that one department will differ from another.

When something doesn't sell at the original price, then mark it down. You want to move it out of stock and reinvest those dollars into fast-moving items or new goods of some sort appropriate for the time period.

This points out the necessity of planning for markdowns in the formal OTB planning process. Leaving out this important occurrence will throw off all other planning such as cash flow and borrowing needs.

Our approach will be to develop OTB plans for a new store. If you are an existing store and would like to organize your previous year's figures for comparison, then use the instructions in Appendix I. I caution you, though, to first feel comfortable with the math and the OTB plan in general before pulling out historical figures from your records to reconstruct into the terms and components here.

CREATING YOUR OTB PLAN

Effective Merchandising Goals:

1. Maximize profit and minimize investment.
2. Realistic planning and implementation of plan.
3. Procurement and maintenance of consumer-satisfying inventory balanced in assortment and depth.

Merchandise planning is basic, simple and logical. Use it—to your advantage—meaning profitably.

To begin your planning process, first work on your sales projections and the stockturn. Since inventory supports sales, you need to know how many times the inventory will turn through the store. This enables you to figure the inventory levels needed and then ultimately your OTB, which maintains the needed stock levels monthly.

The Basic Elements of Your Plan Are:

- Sales
- Stock (Inventory)
- Markdowns
- Purchases

STOCKTURN

Stockturn is a key to beginning your planning as well as for the evaluation of actual figures. Remember, stockturn evaluates the number of times your inventory turns in a year. This is your investment turning a profit if it's fast enough. You won't find any one universal stockturn. Also, stockturn will differ from one department to another, and must be evaluated accordingly. For example, a health food store's various departments turned from five times a year to 16 times a year. Each turn level was appropriate for each different department.

Total Sales	Average Inventory	Annual Turn
268,000	52,000	5.15
439,562	94,788	3.68
174,291	67,525	2.58

Accept for now that the number of times your inventory turns in the store is based on an average inventory carried throughout the year. Later when we look at analyzing the performance of your store, you will learn how to calculate this figure for yourself. Since this is an annual figure, you use the year's sales.

For a new store, you will use your annual sales projections to calculate stockturn. Working with projections, that will be your store's sales projections for the year. Turn is important, because you make money turning your inventory over as many times as possible. Turn represents a flow of goods through the store. Inventory comes in (like your beginning inventory). Sales reduce inventory. More inventory comes in to refresh the appearance of the store and replace strong-selling merchandise (reorders).

Stockturn appears, as mentioned earlier in the health food store example, as a number (as opposed to a percentage or a fraction). This does not mean it will be only a whole number. A store could turn its total inventory 4.3 times per year. One department in that store could turn 5.5 times per year and another 3.7. You will see this later as we analyze the Sales and Purchase Performance Report.

You can find comparative figures with a little research effort. Try looking at financial reports of specific industries, or best of all, obtain information from industry associations. The local library or a university library with a strong business section will greatly aid this search.

If stores in other areas are willing to talk to you, find out their stockturn. Obtain an idea from them of what the average stock (at retail, of course) is for their store. You will see that there is a relationship between the frequency of purchase and the stock turnover rate. Items purchased frequently by the end user have a higher turnover rate than categories not purchased as frequently. Also, the wider the assortment of style, color, size, etc., the slower the turnover rate. Keep this guideline in mind as you research your own industry.

Our first look at a merchandise plan will be for a total store. **Each department in your store should have its own plan and evaluation reports.** In buying, planning and evaluating at any time period, remember that any store or department does not have a constant stock level. We're not referring to just daily but month to month (plans are set up monthly). This is where many people find confusion when learning to calculate Open To Buy. Just as sales at different times of the year fluctuate, so do stock levels—but not proportionately!

Clear your mind of any other notions you have of figuring stock levels. In particular, avoid just going to market and buying what you think is going to sell (dollar-wise or otherwise).

PROJECTING SALES

Now, to continue our journey let's look at the projected sales for the store. Sales projections for a start-up store will be based on many factors:

- Where it is located (geographic and community)
- What type of location (mall, strip center, etc.)
- Type of merchandise
- Competition proximity
- Industry trends
- Economic conditions

These factors also hold true for an existing store planning its increases (or even decreases for a department).

Let's look at an example:

Hot Tomato Designs plans to do $250,000 in its first year of business. From researching banking figures, association reports and such, the owners feel comfortable projecting a stockturn of 4.5 for the total store. Departmental breakdowns vary from 1.75 to 5, but we'll just look at the total store for now.

Average Inventory Calculation

$$\frac{\text{Sales for the Year}}{\text{Stock Turn}} = \text{Average Inventory}$$

$$\frac{\$250,000}{4.5} = \$55,556$$

As we use stockturn and other figures, you will see that the plan actually balances planned sales and planned stock. The control is the Open To Buy figure itself. Before calculating the OTB, we must know the Stock to Sales Ratio (S/S Ratio). Use the Average BOM figure just calculated to find the S/S Ratio.

Calculating the S/S Ratio

$$\frac{\text{AVG. BOM} \times 13}{\text{SALES}} = \text{S/S RATIO}$$

$$\frac{\$55,556 \times 13}{\$250,000} = 2.89$$

Please don't be boggled by the multiplication of the BOM by 13. To figure all the inventory to be handled in a year properly, you need all 12 BOM figures plus the EOM at the end of the year. Thus we can more accurately arrive at the average S/S Ratio figure.

Understanding the S/S Ratio

Remember there needs to be enough stock to **support** sales. I didn't say that sales justify inventory. That decision comes about due to particular sales situations.

If you're out of an item or low on selection, the customer goes elsewhere. Yes, we are talking about a delicate balance. **That doesn't preclude the fact that inventory actually supports sales of items in the total merchandise assortment when at the proper depth.**

How so?

1. If stock is not balanced due to out-of-stock situations, you've just made servicing the customer more difficult for you and your staff.

2. Overstocking of items within a class to total store reduces turnover. Lower turn equals lower profits.

Considerations that Influence Planned BOM

1. Assortment of Merchandise. You need adequate merchandise in sufficient quantity to cover sales until replacement stock hits. You can detail your dollar stock plan with classifications, price lines, types, colors, sizes, etc.

2. Anticipated (projected) Sales. Your goals are to realize stockturn, minimize markdowns, and have a flow of new goods steadily moving throughout the month.

(Ship dates and other delivery aspects in ordering to assist in achieving this goal are discussed in Chapter 2, The Purchase Order.)

Stocks fluctuate with seasonal sales, reaching a peak just before that period of peak sales. You then decrease BOM as a season comes to a close, when customer demand decreases.

From this, we can conclude that our store example in the calculation on the previous page won't have a S/S Ratio of 2.89 every month. July may be 2.7 and December 1.8. The S/S Ratio of 2.89 is the annual average figure that guides you in the planning stage and helps you evaluate later on when comparing actual figures to plan figures.

To calculate an OTB, use the annual S/S Ratio (which is the overall store average) as the starting point. We will also consider the S/S Ratio on a seasonal basis and, of course, monthly, since the plan will figure each month for a full year. The seasonal consideration means in terms of whether it is a peak time, on the upswing or downturn.

Generally, the S/S Ratio is higher at slower months than busier months. When demand is at a peak, a higher (or the highest) number of customers is going through your store and the desire to buy is high. Your stock selection will be good, but so will customer buying—therefore, you don't need the high S/S Ratio to create sales. Study of the OTB plan example will explain this further because you can fully see the flow of goods.

Existing stores can refer to Appendix I for calculations of historical figures to have historical S/S Ratios for comparison. Again, if you are a novice to dollar inventory planning, wait to do this until after you feel comfortable with the OTB plan itself.

Let's now look at the example OTB plan. Hot Tomato Designs is an upper priced fashion store in a strip center located in an upper middle to upper income area with a mix of apartment buildings and homes (translate this information into density of population and a mix of life-styles).

CALCULATING OTB USING S/S RATIO

In this method of figuring how much merchandise to bring in each month, we calculate the BOM inventory using the S/S Ratio. Multiply the S/S Ratio by the sales projection for the month to arrive at the beginning inventory.

S/S Ratio x Projected Sales = BOM

Consider the flow of goods throughout the store. Goods sell, new merchandise arrives and some goods in the store are marked down to improve their sell through. OK. The BOM for any month (at the first of the month) will also be the EOM from the previous month. As goods sell down the inventory, you need new inventory to build to the BOM needed for the next month.

As you figure the OTB with the various formulas this will appear most logical to you. Here are the figures we will be using for Hot Tomato Designs:

Month	Sales	S/S Ratio	Month	Sales	S/S Ratio
Sept	$12,000	4.00	Mar	$21,000	2.85
Oct	$15,000	3.25	Apr	$23,000	3.00
Nov	$22,000	2.10	May	$24,000	2.80
Dec	$42,000	1.80	June	$22,000	2.70
Jan	$18,000	2.65	July	$17,000	2.70
Feb	$18,000	3.90	Aug	$19,000	2.75
			Sept	$19,000	3.00

Indeed, you noticed that the figures begin with a month not at the beginning of either the calendar year or the traditional retailing year of February through January. This store in our example is a start-up and it will open the beginning of September to take advantage of building the business going into the holiday season. The thirteenth month will be explained shortly.

Department Month	Sept	Oct	Nov	Dec	Jan	Feb	Mar
S/S Ratio	4.00	3.25	2.1	1.8	2.65	3.9	2.85
Proj. Sales	12,000	15,000	22,000	42,000	18,000	15,000	21,000
BOM	48,000	48,750	46,200	75,600	47,700	58,500	59,850
Proj. MDs	1,500	1,100	2,100	6,300	2,250	2,520	
EOM (before OTB)	34,750	32,650	22,100	27,300	27,450	40,980	38,850
OTB	14,000	13,550	53,500	20,400	31,050	18,870	

Forms for you to copy to figure your own OTB are presented in the back of this book. First let's look at how to do the calculation.

Next Month's BOM - (BOM - Sales - Markdowns) = OTB

Steps to Figure Your OTB

1. Calculate all BOM by multiplying the Projected Sales by the S/S Ratio.

2. Subtract Sales and Markdown from the current month's BOM (the formula in the parentheses).

3. Subtract the resulting figure from the next month's BOM figure.

Remember: Sales and markdowns reduce the inventory.

To create the sales in the next month the inventory must then be built up to a specific level. Now you can understand why the seventh month sales figure and S/S Ratio appeared in calculating six months of OTB.

Looking at our example store:

Sept Sales = $12,000

Sept S/S ratio 4.00

Sept Markdowns = $ 0

Sept BOM = $48,000

Oct BOM = $48,750

Oct. BOM - (Sept. BOM - Sept. Sales - Sept. MDs) = Sept. OTB

(Or)

$48,750 - ($48,000 - $12,000) = $12,750

An **alternate calculation** of planned purchases adds together all of the reductions along with the amount of inventory needed for the next month and subtracts the current month's beginning inventory figure we are working with. For example:

Projected Sales + Planned Markdowns + Planned EOM (BOM
for next month) - Planned BOM = Planned Purchases at Retail (OTB)

Sept. Sales + Oct. BOM - Sept. BOM = Sept. OTB

Or: $12,000 + $48,750 - $48,000 = $12,750

No, this isn't magic. **Planning purchases (your OTB) facilitates the process, you, the buyer, must go through to maintain a balance between the inventory you carry and your sales.**

The OTB figure is your control figure to maintain that balance. This assists the evaluation of your store at any point in time. We will look at ways to use this control figure at any time during a month's business.

Remember that merchandise planning must by based on planned sales, inventory and markdowns.

USING BASIC STOCK TO FIGURE OTB

Earlier in our preparation of Hot Tomato Design's merchandise plan, we figured the Average Inventory. We can use this to figure a basic stock that must be maintained monthly and then use that to calculate the beginning stock.

First, calculate the Average Inventory and then the Average Sales figures.

Average Inventory = Projected Sales ÷ Annual Stock Turn

$250,000 ÷ 4.5 = $55,556

Average Sales = Projected Sales ÷ 12 Months

$250,000 ÷ 12 = $20,833

Basic Stock = Average Inventory - Average Sales

Basic Stock = $55,556 - $20,833

Basic Stock = $34,723

BOM = Average Inventory + Planned Sales

Department Month	Sept	Oct	Nov	Dec	Jan	Feb	Mar
Proj. Sales	12,000	15,000	22,000	42,000	18,000	15,000	21,000
BOM	46,723	49,723	56,723	76,723	52,723	49,723	55,723
EOM (before OTB)	34,723	34,723	34,723	34,723	34,723	34,723	
OTB	15,000	22,000	42,000	18,000	15,000	21,000	

When you play with the BOM inventory figured in this manner and the remaining formula you will see that the remaining stock before replenishment will always be the Basic Stock. I am not trying to confuse you, but I hope to get you to play with the figures to obtain a better feel for them. This example did not use the markdown figures for the sake of simplicity.

Calculating the OTB will always be the same formulas whether you use S/S Ratios or Basic Stock to calculate the BOM figure. A quick way to do this method of figuring OTB would look like this:

Next Month's BOM - Basic Stock $ = OTB

Play with it. Use the numbers as a way to sharpen the rest of your good business sense.

I have seen both methods plus others used in texts and by all sorts of retailers. I advise understanding the S/S Ratio and using it as your main merchandise planning method. When it comes to doing inventory management and evaluation, you have a better understanding of exactly what has actually occurred with your inventory. In recording data and calculating other formulas for analysis and to take action, you need every tool possible.

Allow yourself time to do your planning. You review merchandise to bring into your store far in advance of any one month. These are the tools used throughout the retailing world by all stores. Use it to your advantage and grow as they have done.

ADDITIONAL MERCHANDISE PLAN ELEMENT GUIDELINES

Use these guidelines to start your plans and to revise them. An OTB plan takes thought as well as time. Pulling numbers out of the air will not benefit you.

Sales Projections

- Examine internal and external factors that could affect sales (see next section for further discussion)
- Study trends in your industry
- Evaluate competition
- Evaluate your own store's sales trends (by department as well as the whole). Existing stores should go back two and three years.
- Calculate the percent contribution of each department to the total store.

Remember, the best plans are specific and flexible.
Aggressiveness pays off.

ELEMENTS AFFECTING YOUR STORE

Many things affect a business. They fall into one of two categories, either internal or external. The following presents a breakdown of these factors to assist in your merchandise planning.

External Factors

- Economy and general consumer outlook (optimistic or not, or perhaps flat)
- Demographic changes (increase in one section of population over another, like low-income over high-income)
- Pending strikes

- City plans for street construction
- Employment prospects in the area
- New competition, competition closing, new mall(s)
- Other new businesses in the area that increase the population, like a large office building
- New residential areas or decline in same
- Changes in streets, access to your center or parking facilities
- Changes in technology
- Social and cultural activities (can be related to life-style psychographics)
- Political trends and activities

Internal Factors

- Changes in staff
- Changes in physical appearance of your store
- Expansion of your store to additional units
- Sales trends
- Changes in promotion/marketing plan

REWORKING YOUR OTB PLAN

Project 12 months of sales broken down into monthly sales goals. This keeps you thinking about where you are going. A psychologist once said that dreams not written down will always remain dreams. I truly believe this and have found it to be true when working with clients.

I evaluate each month on its own, then add them up for the 12-month projection and then rework. I do this for total store and each department. After adjusting the departments, tally up the S/S Ratio for the 12 months in each department, divide by 12 to get the average S/S Ratio. Then add all the average S/S Ratios for the departments to check that you are in line with your projected average S/S Ratio for the total store.

The same goes for sales if you revise them at all. Your purpose is to evaluate the trend of each month for the type of store. Computer programs make this easier (see pages 153-155 for information on a program that does this).

Example: A shoe store's biggest month is August, and not December!

So? What does this mean for the store planning its OTB?

Think about these points. The largest selection needs to be in the store for the back-to-school period since this will be the highest selling time. The S/S Ratio will be lower at that time. When you work on the different departments of the store, it would make sense to not have a heavy stock of holiday shoes. Your local demographics will have told you what age brackets live near your store so you can target them with the proper selection in your inventory.

Remember to step back and work hard at developing an objective view based on the internal and external factors studied.

Also, don't forget one of your most valuable sources of information—your sales staff. They speak to customers all day long. Get their input. This will set you apart from other employers, especially the larger stores who almost never ask their store personnel what they think.

Here is another example:

For a gift store in a seasonal area (like a store in a center affected by conventions or one at a lake resort)—with months that have the heavier traffic certainly needs to evaluate them for sales projections higher than the off-season months.

Think through some of the steps you might take to work on the store's plans.

- Get information from your landlord or convention bureau on the conventions booked. (I suggest the landlord because some bureaus won't deal directly with the merchant but will deal with the merchant's associations or property management companies.)
- If weather is important to your area (such as at a lake resort), did the past year have problems or was it unseasonably great? Perhaps good weather came early, giving you a jump on the season. You may want to be cautious about planning too heavy for the same month in the coming year.
- What types of merchandise looked like they were not as popular as before? Does there seem to be a trend in a department? Do you see any type of goods that could replace the slow-selling merchandise?

Other examples of different product seasons would be toys and furs with their own unique seasons.

Don't assume in planning. Don't use hearsay that appears as fact.

We hear certain "facts" so many times that they seem true. Research puts you into a position of strength and gives you the information needed to make your buying decisions.

ADDITIONAL THOUGHT PROCESSES IN PROJECTING SALES

Consider holidays in relation to your type of merchandise, your planned promotions, last year's promotions, your notes on problems last year such as a plague of bad deliveries in one month, weather or construction that affected your area or shopping center and last year's market conditions (not stock market but the overall source of your goods).

Keep a store calendar/record book where you record each day's sales, last year's sales, promotions running on that day, weather conditions, situations that arrive and so on. Use this book for reference when you do your planning and evaluate possible increases or decreases in sales. More about how to put together a "Figures to Beat" book and ideas for using it appear in the chapter on Buying Strategies.

For a new store, consult other merchants in the area and the shopping center you're considering, your banker and vendors to obtain information to help you formulate your projections.

From the definition of the target market you can then develop the many components making up the basis for the store image and merchandising policies.

Making Your Plans More Specific

Now that you have been through the math portion of the OTB plan, you can apply some parameters to make your plan specific for your store. Policies affect your store in many aspects. Write them out to assist in guiding the business and for all of your staff to know—at least write down those that relate to your philosophy for the business and carrying out the function of the business.

Policies for Planning

- Price range
- Quality standards
- Breadth and depth of assortment
- Brand offerings
- Exclusivity—whether you offer it or not
- Relationship to fashion trends—a leader, follower or somewhere in between
- Basic stock maintenance—your store doesn't carry basics, always carries them, or only depending on the season

The following considerations for each point will help you develop policies for your store. Spend time thinking and rethinking them in terms of your store concept and target market. Specific techniques, "how-to's" and examples are presented in the chapter on Merchandising Techniques. This overview will fuel the thought process needed to develop your own OTB plans.

Price

Consider your target market's income. Remember that price and quality don't always go hand in hand. Decisions in price affect all other areas, policies and activities of the store, such as: layout, customer service, size of store, type of goods carried, ads and promotions, visual merchandising and so on. (Discounting is a price choice.)

Quality

The range of quality in workmanship, style, and materials should not be overlooked in this process. Would you include irregulars in your assortment? Or as special promos only?

Depth and Breadth Assortment

Only a few styles in the product mix means that colors and sizes are **narrow and deep**. The selection of styles being narrow allows the store to offer depth in colors and sizes. This makes for a larger selection for everyone in those few styles if you follow this mix technique.

A lot of styles in the product selection means that the selection is made up of only selected colors and sizes **broad and shallow**. The style selection comprises the breadth of the product mix with a shallow selection of colors or sizes.

These terms "narrow and deep" and "broad and shallow" pertain to a lot more than just clothing colors and styles. Try visualizing assortments of towels, dolls, home accessories, stationery items and so on. Relate this to your store concept to ask yourself, "Does my customer prefer the variety in selecting styles and/or items over a few styles with a large color and/or feature variety?"

Narrow assortments help develop a small store's image quickly, communicating to your customer what type of store you are and what to expect from you.

Brand Offerings

National names such as Levi's, Liz Claiborne, Hanes, Thomasville, Reebok, Craftsman, Sherwin Williams, Weyerhauser, Corning, Noritake and so on create a recognition response by the consumer. Do not assume that it will always be a positive response. If your customers prefer to set their own style and statement, this may not be a good buying policy for your store.

Other types of brand offerings:

Private Label: You put your label on items purchased from a vendor or manufactured specifically for you. This is a large dollar commitment most independents cannot do for a few years into their operation. However, ask vendors when you are at market what kind of programs or other offerings they have to put your name on a product. Some industries do not require large initial purchases.

Signature: Endorsed private label like Krizia in the Limited stores.

Designer: Just that, a recognized designer item.

Exclusivity

An exclusive product deal with a vendor is difficult to do for a small store. You must know your financial position before committing yourself to any exclusivity with a manufacturer.

If you feel comfortable in doing this, here are some points to follow:

- Ask for one or more styles to be confined to your store.
- Work with new manufacturers or designers, etc., in your trading areas. Those new businesses are more willing to work with buyers to get their name out and to build their business.
- Seek out new sources noting your competitor's stores.
- Look for private designs manufacturing (though large quantities are needed).

Be careful here. The dollar amount needed to do your label could stifle your business or at worst ruin you. There are companies that specialize in private label who have their own design staff. This way, they have the design commitment, not you, making it a safer bet. You can have them put your label into the garments you select. Since companies come and go, check with a resident buying office to find such a company and follow your trade magazines.

- Investigate licensing. This does not refer to a private label but using another's name or product. There are whole trade shows devoted to licensing products, and it is a complicate form of business. Again, seek information and aid in negotiations from a resident buying office known for this.

For the most part, using exclusivity to build your store's image takes more than just the commitment from the vendor and your dollars. Your commitment in planning carefully for promotions, communications and development are crucial. You must know your exact financial commitment and what you can afford to lose if it doesn't work out. Timing plays an important factor as you need an appropriate amount of time to communicate to your customers when instituting this policy. Too little time won't give you a good readout on customer response, hence the risk in marketing dollars as well as inventory purchases

Product Relationship to Fashion Trends

Where to be positioned on the cycle emphasizes your image. Cycles of trends are the reference point here. Some people wait to "jump on the band wagon" while others must be on the cutting edge with new innovations. Look at the Sharper Image product mix for a good example of the latter type of customer.

Trends and cycles exist in much more than just the clothing and accessory industries, as we now see in adult "toys" (Nintendo), luggage, travel (China after Nixon and safaris), household goods like cookware with the health awareness and changing styles of cooking coming out of California (Alice Waters' restaurant, Chez Panisse).

This points out the need to read and be aware of the business environment and changes in life styles. Read, observe and research!

Understand that where you want to be on the cycle relates to your target market.

Basic Stock Maintenance

Basic stock is an item in consistent demand creating the need to be in stock in a complete range of sizes, colors or other pertinent selection criteria, such as mugs with graphics on them if that's what your customer continually buys.

Classification Breakdown

Thoroughly think out how your merchandise should be broken down into departments and subclasses. You need trend information in groupings that tell you more than just the sales amount. That would be pointless and a waste of your planning efforts. Look closely at some of the examples cited in this chapter and future chapters. They provide the guidelines for you to create your own department and subclass breakdowns into meaningful components.

Customer Service Policies and Offerings

What additional services should you offer to emphasize your concept and set you apart from the competition?

Services in small stores help you out-merchandise the larger chains. Give this a lot of time and effort in development and be sure it is communicated to the customer in every way possible. An independent retailer can offer personal touches not found in department stores and most large specialty chains. Things as simple as offering gift wrapping, special orders and referral services make a customer feel special and enjoy the shopping experience a lot more than at other stores.

These services may not seem that much in comparison to the competition or "the big boys." It's true. Look around you and you will see that other retailers are offering more than ever before. You need to as well. Most important, when competing with retailers of any size, you must communicate what you offer the customer. Communicate it with signs, yes, but most of all with your sales people. You are more than a retailer now, you are a trainer. You must continually train your people and repeat store polices. This creates consistency. If every salesperson will say the same thing, there is no possibility for confusion for the customer. (See Chapter 5 for information on staff and selling skills).

However, not offering special services will make you less than a "me-too" store. You'll soon find yourself without customers. To develop a set of services, go through the following list. Brainstorm how you can use these to make your products and store customized in comparison to your competitors.

- Guarantees and warranties
- Training in how to use a product
- Technical advice or technical support
- Showing customers alternative uses for products
- Supply replacement parts
- Newsletter
- Follow-up customer purchase for evaluation
- Product user clubs, collector clubs
- Monitor product performance after purchase

ACTION LIST FOR CHAPTER 1

- Write out target market and customer profiles.
- Plan out department breakdown for store along with subclasses.
- Decide on price range by department.
- List your competition and the voids you will fill.
- Write out your store concept.
- Project first year sales for the total store. Do your first year sales projections for each department and calculate each department's percent of the total store sales.

• Project desired annual stockturn and average inventory for store and departments.

• Use basic stock or S/S Ratio to plan at least a six-month OTB. (Calculate average sales if using basic stock method.)

• Write out desired product assortments for each department.

• Go though external and internal factors list and write out for each point the elements affecting your store.

• Identify any brands you want to carry.

Chapter 2

The Purchase Order: The Form And Its Use

Most independent retailers use the manufacturers' Purchase Orders (PO). The purchase order is one of the important documents used in your purchasing system.

Let me suggest that you use your own form. Here's why:

- It supports a professional image to vendors.

- All terms are communicated and understood.

- You can read copies in your system easily and find information quickly instead of hunting for information on unfamiliar forms.

- You will reduce or eliminate unauthorized purchases.

- It facilitates the receiving process, when you verify a PO against a packing slip and later to the invoice.

- It communicates pertinent information to employees like retail price, department and subclass numbers.

A copy of a Purchase Order is in the back of the book (see p. 142). You can design your own, accommodating any special product needs or instructions. The following list discusses the items that should appear on your Purchase Order to make it a complete and useful document in your system.

ITEMS ON THE PO

Date of Order: Place the date of the original communication, not when the PO is written or typed. I used to order or reorder over the phone and give the vendor a PO number. At that time, I entered the date, style numbers and quantities ordered. Later I filled in the rest from notes including descriptions of items.

Vendor: Write in name and address of seller, not the manufacturer's representative or "rep." The vendor will invoice you and that is the party this contract affects.

Ship To: Most likely, your store address and shipping address are the same. If you have more than one location and wish to ship to each one, then indicate here about the split. You can write the store shipping instructions in the body of the PO, but you may eventually print a PO with a store distribution chart on it.

Delivery Date Or Ship Date: I strongly recommend using a specific date. Most retailers enter A/R for "As Ready" because the rep always says it. If you intend to manage your inventory, then you tell the vendor when to ship to you. Otherwise, manufacturers can beef up their receivables by shipping an item that hit their warehouses early, which could be two months before you need it. Think of the seasonal goods that would get old and become markdowns because they hit your store too early.

To Arrive: This and the Cancel Date may be the same or the arrive date could be stated in terms of "week of."

F.O.B. "Free On Board": In traffic language really means:

1. At what point the buyer takes legal title to the goods.
2. Who is responsible for making claims against the carrier.

Most small businesses utilize one of two terms:

1. F.O.B. Destination (your store)
2. F.O.B. Shipping Point (the vendor's plant)

Freight—Prepaid or Collect: If freight is prepaid, then you pay the vendor the freight on the invoice. If collect, then you pay the freight company directly.

Terms: How will the vendor receive payment from you? Fill in (or circle) the seller's terms or those negotiated.

Item Number: The vendor's stock/style number of the item itself.

Description: Describe the item purchased. If there has been a misunderstanding, the vendor can catch it. Also, your employees can easily identify goods when checking them in. If you go over future shipments with employees, you won't have to sort through your notes from market.

Unit Description: Specify if the item being purchased is by the dozen, case or each.

*Specify the cost per unit from the manufacturer/vendor and per piece cost for your pricing.

PURCHASE ORDER

DATE: SEPT 1, 1993   P.O.# 0010203

TO: Tot Tailors   SHIP/BILL: Elite Small Shop

     1350 Broadway   704 Cameron Way

     NY, NY 10010   Elm Tree Center

         Olive City, CA 93045

TERMS: *SHIPPING INSTRUCTIONS*   Carrier: UP

2/10 N 30   Start Ship Date: <u>OCT 15, 1993</u>

F.O.B. <u>STORE</u>   To Arrive: _____

         Cancel Date: <u>NOV 5, 1993</u>

Misc. Instructions:

     no trucks allowed to deliver at mall between 11:30 and 1:00

# D/Sub	Description	Qty.	Unit	Cost	Tot. $	Retl.	R.Tot	
1014	red stripe overalls	6	ea.	11—	66.—			

This constitutes the information for the vendor's copy. After you send off the original, fill out the rest. Having the retail prices along with departmental and subclass information immediately available for an employee makes everyone's job easier when checking in merchandise.

A purchase order is a contract, so treat it with the same respect you would give any other legal document.

A note about confirming orders—many times, orders get placed over the phone. You need the PO for your own internal controls, but it is worth the time and the effort to send a copy to the vendor. Now, you've given the vendor or rep the PO number over the telephone, but that isn't enough to prevent duplication. Write "Confirming order—DO NOT Duplicate" across the PO.

Also write the name of the person you talked with. The shipping department then has someone to go to for any problems. This saves aggravation for everyone involved.

For additional safety, have printed on the order under the signature "No changes can be made to purchase order without written authorization from above person." This protects you in a shipping dispute, especially if they substitute a style you ordered with another style. Chances are that you won't want it. This statement allows you the stance of demanding to return it without question.

Extend the costs, total the order, then send it to the vendor. This facilitates auditing vendor invoices before payment and your cash flow management.

Various refinements of terms follow this next section. More detailed discussions of terms and how to use them in your business and buying strategy appear in other chapters.

THE PURCHASING SYSTEM

For most stores, a four-part Purchase Order provides a complete system to deal with merchandising and OTB planning and inventory management to the accounting side of your business. Even in the most organized firms, PO copies can disappear for no reason. Using a four-part PO allows for efficient handling of goods and backup. A large organization may even move to a five-part, using the fifth copy for numerical control.

In this age of technological advances, most of us think that a system means computers. Something as informal as putting sales slips on a spindle and tallying at some time of the day before filing them constitutes a system. Bank deposits, customer file procedures and the like also are system applications in your company. If you do something consistently, you have created a system for your store.

A system is comprised of four stages:

- Input
- Processing
- Outputs
- Feedback

In the context of purchasing, you:

1. Recognize the need for stock, new or a reorder—Input.

2. Fulfill the need by selecting the vendor, items, terms, etc., and enter and order—Processing.

3. Place an order with the vendor(s)—Output.

4. Watch how the need was fulfilled through sales trends, price evaluation, vendor performance, and so on—Feedback.

Get it? Now let's relate this to your purchasing system and the Purchase Order.

Purchase Orders should be printed with your numbers in consecutive order and with at least three, if not four copies. Four copies is preferred in the following manner: From top to bottom—white, pink, yellow, green.

White copy: The top copy (white) goes to the vendor. The dollar retail amounts do not have to be filled in for the vendor; those columns are for you, the retailer.

  • Fill in all other information, especially the shipping information as discussed previously.

  • A completion date is necessary (or as some call it, the cancel date). This is a contract that you and the vendor are bound by. If goods are not shipped to you on time and arrive past the completion date, you have the right to refuse them. This is one of the areas that is important in regards to controlling inventory. The vendors may call you to extend the completion date if they are running late in delivery. A decision to "OK" the extension is based on sales in the store and subsequent need for goods and also the importance of the item. If an ad is planned for these goods, or the shipment was a major part of the planned inventory mix, obviously some heavy decision-making is needed.

  • Before separating the remaining copies, be sure to enter the retail price for each item and extend the total retail amount. You now have your data to check against your OTB.

Internal System—The Other Three Copies

Pink: Keep the second copy to track your orders. Watch delivery dates to make sure that merchandise is received when you planned.

  • File these copies by completion date. This allows for easy rechecking in reference to planned inventory levels and follow up with vendors.

  • Use these copies to tally the "on order" figure used with OTB plans.

  • Check this copy against the store copy (yellow/third copy) after goods are received to verify the items. Physical checking of merchandise will be done along the way as goods are received. Color or size ordered may vary from the PO and can be caught by those checking in goods. As a buyer, you want to look for changes you made on the PO that didn't get onto the store copy (third copy) or see if a vendor is shipping you inefficiently. As the store owner, you also want to verify any order before it is paid.

Yellow: The third copy should reside in the store, filed alphabetically as open orders.

- As you receive goods, an employee (or employees) responsible for checking in merchandise will pull the packing slip off of the box to find the vendor's name and PO # the order is shipped against.
- The employee can then go to the file to find the PO. The retail prices along with the department and subclass are on it. The employee does not have to go elsewhere for that information.

- Circle the quantities received if correct. Mark differing amounts on the purchase order accordingly. If you receive goods you didn't order, note it on the packing slip.
- Attach the packing slip and order copy to one another and pass on to the accounting person. This may also go to the buyer to OK an order for payment from the invoice. COD orders obviously do not go through this step, but are immediately filed in the accounting files of paid invoices.
- When accounting receives invoices, they will be matched up to this purchase order copy, attached to the copy you retain and, when paid, filed alphabetically in "accounts paid."

Green: The fourth copy is maintained in a file by vendor name along with all other information on the vendor the buyer feels is necessary to maintain. This copy allows for the buyer to work with a vendor on the phone with all information needed at hand without having to look elsewhere. This is also a back-up if any other copy is misplaced and a valuable cross-reference.

This is a good point to expand on F.O.B. terms. The following chart should help you sort out what is the best way for you and your store to handle shipping and shipment problems.

F.O.B. Terms

F.O.B. Shipping Point, Freight Collect: Everything is on you, the buyer. You take title when the goods are shipped, pay and bear freight charges, and file any claims.

F.O.B. Shipping Point, Freight Allowed: Seller pays and bears freight charges. Buyer (you, the store owner) owns goods in transit and file claims.

F.O.B. Shipping Point, Freight Prepaid and Charges Back: Seller pays freight charges, but buyer bears freight charges. Buyer owns goods and files claims.

F.O.B. Destination, Freight Collect: Buyer pays freight charges. Seller owns goods in transit and files claims.

F.O.B. Destination, Freight Prepaid: Seller pays and bears freight charges. Seller owns goods in transit and files claims.

F.O.B. Destination, Freight Collect and Allowed: Buyer pays freight charges. Seller bears freight charges, owns goods in transit and files claims.

If you negotiate F.O.B. Destination, the onus is upon the Seller to track down the shipment and put your invoice on hold if an order is lost. This saves you time, dollars and hassle.

In my experience, I have found vendors willing to track down orders even if the order stated F.O.B. Shipping Point. They want their invoice to be paid. Be smart and put it on hold until you have evidence of the location of the shipment and a resolution you can live with has been negotiated in the case of a lost shipment.

Many small store owners go to market and place orders in the showroom with reps or vendors before fully shopping the market. I urge my clients to break themselves of the habit of leaving orders in showrooms. Shop your market and know everything you possibly can evaluate goods in relation to your OTB before writing that contract.

Receiving Goods

When packages arrive you and/or your employees can minimize lost paper and problems with a few guidelines.

Cover these points whenever training a new employee to ensure your system is properly employed.

- Utilize one area and the same personnel for receiving if at all practical.
- If a packing slip doesn't exist (very unlikely) use a receiving report—a card or such to document goods received to be compared to the PO.
- Stores with more volume and departmentalized duties benefit from using copies of receiving reports to notify accounting and buyers of the merchandise's arrival.
- Open packages and inspect goods promptly. Avoid complicating a problem due to internal delays, thus giving the vendor the edge in negotiating a resolution.
- Make notes of damages and/or missing boxes on carrier's receipt and packing slip and/or receiving report.
- Process goods and paperwork quickly, preferably in 24 hours.

From time to time you will receive damaged or defective goods, or incorrect or unauthorized (not ordered) goods, overshipments, duplicate shipments, short shipments and so on. The guidelines previously listed play an important part in correcting these types of problems. Again, their purpose is to give you more control over what happens in and to your business.

Returns to Vendors

Most vendors require returns to have a return authorization, which they will issue. Unfortunately, a buyer's time gets fragmented by sloppy vendors when they drag their feet on such problems. Stay on top of them by confirming all conversations in writing. Time consuming? Yes, but worth it in showing a vendor they cannot take advantage of you. Being a small independent retailer does not mean being unimportant business-wise. There are other vendors who are more professional than the company with that jerky rep and poor shipping system you've had to deal with!

Vendor Files

The fourth copy of the PO is the most helpful component in your system. Combined with other information, you save time and show your professionalism by setting up vendor files.

Your vendors are your resources, the pieces you combine to create the whole—your store. Your vendor files allow you to do this more efficiently and have access to information when problems arise.

How to Maintain and Use Vendor Files

Maintain a file for each vendor, current and past. In it keep the materials given to you by the vendor, such as brochures, photos of items, promotional material copies and so on. All of your notes from market also go into this file.

Last but not least, keep the fourth copy of your PO in this file. To make it neat and easy to use, fasten all of the PO copies on the left-hand side of the manila folder. The most recently written copy goes on the top. Photocopies of return authorization stickers go on this side as well. This is a total purchase and inventory record of each vendor in one place.

Situation Example

You're talking to the vendor on the phone verifying the items you want to order. One of the items has been cut from production and the representative you are talking to says that another style or item booked much better and would be better for your store. Look to see if you took a note on this style at market and any comments you made about it. Now you can decide if you believe the information from the vendor or rep about the style for your store.

If you agree, and purchase it, you have just saved yourself the aggravation of placing an order, not receiving it and all of the other machinations you have to go through when an order received does not match the purchase order.

Your vendor file doubles as a backup for any lost paperwork. Unfortunately, no matter how organized you are, some paper slips through our neat systems and disappears. Your vendor file provides a great place to look for an order copy if the receiving copy has been misplaced or even the follow-up file copy is gone.

Communication with a vendor is a lot easier when you have a complete vendor file with all purchase order copies in front of you. If the vendor is on the phone, you will not have to put him or her on hold to find other paper work pertaining to your conversation. You can review vendor activity at a glance.

While you're on the phone, you may see that many styles are returned due to poor quality. (File notes about returns with copies of return authorizations and letters.) Discuss this problem while you have the attention of the vendors. Review the activity with specific vendors before going to market to discuss problems and/or ideas for future business such as ad support.

Now that you are armed with an OTB plan and your PO along with your vendor files it's time to track just what goes on in your store through inventory movement. This is Inventory Management.

ACTION LIST FOR CHAPTER 2

- Make a set of vendor files, sorted alphabetically in a file drawer.
- Make a set of files for order follow-up:

    One file for the current month orders due to come in.

    One file for past due orders not canceled (and still desired)

    One file for future delivery; you can have two files, one for the next 30 days and the other for future deliveries.

- Design or have designed a Purchase Order form with your store logo and name, shipping address, etc. Follow the blank Purchase Order in the Appendix as a guide (see p. 142). Be sure your telephone number is on it and large enough to find and read quickly.

- Check with your attorney about placing any language specific to your business on the PO. This might be declaration of raw materials, packaging parameters or handling of the invoice. Most small stores don't have the buying power to demand the manufacturer package a specific way.

• To help you in market, make a chart of the following information for each vendor, adding new vendors as you work in the market:

F.O.B. point

Terms

Contact or rep name

Telephone number

• Buy an alphabetical file for your receiving copies of Purchase Orders. Place open orders in file for staff to pull when shipments arrive.

Chapter 3

Inventory Management Systems

HOW TO COLLECT YOUR DATA AND MANAGE IT

Inventory Management is the recordkeeping and systems that provide objective data. Decisions are based upon this data—facts, not "eyeball" perceptions. Facts/records are a reliable guide far exceeding the best of memories. To better control your business, you need that objective data to answer questions like these:

- Which vendors are the most profitable?
- What departments have a higher turn?
- Do certain sizes or colors sell better than others?
- What percentage does each department contribute to the whole?
- What is the cumulative markon in each department?
- Do some of your vendors have a high rate of return to the vendor indicating poor quality or disregard for your shipping instructions?
- What trends are indicated by sales? By markdowns?
- What is your dollar inventory at any one point in time? You always have a control figure to check shrinkage, as well as for when you take a full store inventory.

Without records you are stabbing in the dark with your best guess."Black and white" figures stare back at you with what you need to know about consumer demand. Interpreting these facts correctly, and consistently enables you to meet your customers' wants and needs.

Independent retailers use a system for a variety of reasons:

- No longer efficient to eyeball
- Staying competitive with the right buys, timely markdowns, timely purchases (with cash you'll have with planning)
- Control and understanding of cash flow
- Better records aid in developing your relationship with banks
- Increased negotiating ability with vendors by having actual records vs. just saying to vendor, "We didn't do very well with you last year" (your competitor is ahead of you with records and negotiating power).

• Having a system in place prepares you for growth as sales increase. This cuts costs in your own learning and instituting new systems later; lower training costs of personnel because you know the procedures. You won't have to learn along with your staff; this also increases your image as the authority and leader in the organization.

• Reduces problems in opening new, additional stores; this can also happen sooner with your inventory under control.

COLLECTING YOUR DATA

Once my clients begin to see how valuable the information is in helping them make their buying and other merchandising decisions, the question of "Why?" disappears

The first reaction I get from most people is, "I already have an accountant." You can see from the math we have gone through that this is not what your accountant will do for you. The second reaction is, "I don't have enough time." Do you have the time to run your business and make a profit? Well, then you have time. You'll have more time when you go back to working for someone else if you don't work on your inventory management.

What to Track and Record?

The OTB plan you are now familiar with includes information you need in some form or another. The following lists inventory movement you need to record.

- Price changes—both markdowns and markons
- Purchases
- Returns to vendor
- Sales
- Transfers

These components interact through various formulas in the "Sales and Purchases Performance Report." This Merchandising Information Report provides the data needed to truly manage and control inventory.

KNOW WHAT IS SELLING

The all consuming figure for everyone is SALES. To everyone, it means cash in the bank, customers coming through the door, productive marketing ideas and profit. We'll begin here, looking at ways to know what has sold, on our journey through Inventory Management.

For a moment, we'll assume that the dark ages still exist and that you do not have an Electronic Cash Register (ECR). Most small, independent stores are not going to opt for a computer based "Point of Sale" register especially since ECRs have become quite sophisticated. Many now have the ability to have a communications board installed in them to allowing a computer to "talk" to the ECR. The figures are pulled into simple report formats. With an ECR, you program prices and stock numbers (either Price Look Ups and/or Stock Keeping Units), program discounts and so forth, keeping such functions out of the hands of $5 an hour sales staff.

If you didn't have a cash register, you would have to collect your sales from sales tickets written at the time of the sale. Of course, sales slips get lost, or a salesperson throws it away on purpose, pocketing the cash for themselves. Another problem is the time-consuming task of writing all of this out on your daily tally sheet and adding up the results. Manual data collection is simply not as accurate as other methods.

In the forms available, in Appendix III, the Daily Tally Sheet appears. Here is a portion filled out. As you see in the form, you fill in the code number of an item when it appears for the first time. Add hash marks for additional sales of the item. Depending on the level of sales your store produces, fill out this form daily or weekly. The total for the month is added up for each department and entered on the Sales and Purchase Performance Report. (An interior design/furniture store may choose to do this weekly since the number of sales would not be high, even though the dollar amounts would be.)

Enter the retail price of the item, not the price with the sales tax added onto it. The code number lets you spot reorder items.

DAILY TALLY SHEET

Department <u>Ceramics-05</u>   Subclass <u>Vases - 42</u>   Week/Month <u>3/20 - 3/26</u>

Date	Code #	Vendor	Description	Price	Tally	Qty.	Total Dollars
3/20		Top Hat	cut crystal	52—	//	2	104.00
3/20	43588	Divine	porcelain bud	18—	////	4	72.00
3/21	75588	Jeri Lynn	carved teak	39—	///	3	117.00
3/21		Top Hat	cut crystal	27—	///	3	81.00

If you use the other form without the code number, the retail price is the identifier. Tracking by departments with or without subclasses in this method also has the vendor name/code to help identify an item.

Let me explain with an example. Two items have sold in the "Plush" department of your children's toy store. One item sells for $29 and the other $36. They are entered on separate lines since they are different prices even though they are in the same department. Now, as you go through your sales slips at the end of the day you come across another item in "Plush" that sold for $29 with the same vendor name. You place a hash mark next to the other one you marked for the first $29 item.

Do these entries daily. You don't want to chance misplacing sales slips. Share this job with different people on your sales staff. This encourages their feedback and gives you some security control (not much, but some). Add up the hash marks in the "Tally" column and enter the number in the "Quantity Sold" column. Then multiply the "Quantity Sold" times the "Price Sold" to arrive at the "Total Dollars."

At the end of the day, total each department to get a grand total for the day, which you will enter in your "Figures to Beat" book; weekly add up each department and enter it on a weekly recap sheet with marketing and other pertinent information. The monthly totals will be entered on the "Sales and Purchase Performance Report" with many other merchandising figures and calculations.

The Daily Tally Sheet lists a column for your own internal stock (code) number. An internal numbering system assists this process.

Ring binders are the best place for keeping your tally sheet. They're available for you, the buyer, to glance at for highlights. Hot selling areas stick out quickly to you with their many scratches of hash marks—showing you in "black and white" what is going on in your business. OK. Piece of cake. Let's get more complicated.

With a simple cash register on your counter you've moved out of the dark ages into the middle ages. Congratulations! You have a big calculator on your counter to dust. If the machine can't track at least 15 departments (and is expandable), have a couple of clerk keys, a couple of tax keys and other basic functions, and possibly alphanumeric capability (which means it will print out names of departments, your store name, etc.) you will outgrow it so fast it won't be funny.

Really, be serious. You're here to make a profit and old clichés about scrimping on pennies apply in this situation. Many of my clients felt like kicking the cash register, but not because it didn't work. It wasn't worth the few hundred dollars they spent, even though they thought they were saving an extra few hundred dollars.

A second tally sheet appears here as another example of tracking your sales. This one has eliminated a code/stock number and put in its place 1) Department/Subclass number and 2) Vendor number (instead of writing a name). At the top is a line to enter the date of the beginning of the week. Your cash register or sales slips give you the figures to enter here.

DAILY TALLY SHEET

Week of: 3/20 - 3/26

Date	Dept./ Sub#	Vendor #	Item Description	Price Sold	Hash Count (Tally)	Qty. Sold	Total Dollars
3/20	03/27		card	1.25	⅃ᴴ⅃ᴴ ⅃ᴴ ⅃ᴴ ⅃ᴴ ⅃ᴴ ///	14	17.5
3/20	03/22		notepad	4.95	⅃ᴴ ⅃ᴴ I	11	54.4
3/20	03/28		stickers	1.75	⅃ᴴ ////	9	15.75
3/21	03/22	104	notepad kit	2.25	⅃ᴴ ⅃ᴴ ⅃ᴴ I	16	36.00

Now, why is this sheet different? The store that benefits from using this form doesn't have items that will reorder. That's right—not all stores live by reorder, but new styles and types of merchandise revolve through the store instead. The key here is breaking down the departments into meaningful subclasses to give you trend information. That is how you will tap into your customer's wants and needs. Earlier we gave the example of a clothing store carrying dresses that were then divided into various subclasses. Here are a few other examples:

A Book Store -
   Department - Health Related
   Subclasses -
      Herb Remedies
      Nutritional
      Diets
      Encyclopedias
      Special Diet Cookbooks
      Informational
A Gift Store -
   Department - Ceramics
   Subclasses -
      Consignment Artists
      Masks
      Vases and Containers
      Statues and Figurines

Interior Design Shop

Department - Small Decorative Items
Subclasses -
Silver
Dried Floral
Picture Frames
Brass
Pillows
Artificial Food

Let's look closer at a situation using subclass demarcation. You are a gift store owner/buyer at market and several of your reps said that porcelain masks were the next hottest trend. As a buyer, you make the decision that your customer has always responded to new trends and that the selection in the market was good. You choose the best styles and decide to place more than a test order quantity.

The merchandise comes in and is ticketed with its own subclass number under the Ceramic Department. You now track the sales trend of this merchandise.

Totaling the tally sheet for the Ceramic Department at the end of the first week shows that a total of three masks sold.

You might remember how many were received from the different vendors, but if you're a busy store and sales staff unpacked all the deliveries this week, that information must be recorded somewhere, right? Of course, that's what this chapter is all about!

After checking the purchases received in that department and subclass, you find a total of 12 pieces received from three different vendors. Using vendor numbers on your items lets you track for reorders. Instead of reordering the same styles, ask that vendor what they have that is similar. This is appropriate, keeping with the need for new styles flowing through the store. The masks were good, but you don't want to bore your customers.

Either tally sheet, or a combination of them, may work for you depending on your store. Defining your store concept and target market (as discussed in Chapter 6, Buying Strategies) is key in choosing which forms to use.

Using an ECR in Your System

If you purchase an ECR with both the capabilities of programming SKUs and PLUs, you have the making of quickly retrievable and usable information. SKUs don't have prices programmed along with the number. (With PLUs, the price is programmed in the ECR so you only enter the PLU number itself.) This allows you to use a SKU number for a subclass. After entering that number (from the label or tag on the item), the ECR will prompt you to enter the price. The price is then keyed in using the number pad and hitting the appropriate department key. The ECR gives you a "read out" of department totals daily. SKU and/or PLU reports are pulled out as you wish.

Using PLUs for items you anticipate having high sales and reorders gives you flexibility. You can retrieve specific information for your business. Isn't life great?

ECRs with lots of programmable keys and department keys have PLU programmability. Opting for a still better ECR gives you SKUs and more information sorted out for you into "reports." These reports are totals grouped together for you. That's right—no more daily tally sheets. You enter totals directly onto the Sales and Purchase Performance Reports and/or weekly recap sheets and your deposit reconciliation forms.

More Detailed Tracking:
Information of Styles/Items—by the Piece

Tracking sales by units is the method called Perpetual Inventory. This means you know at any one time exactly how many of an item you (should) have in stock. The movement of an item is continually recorded by number of units: beginning inventory, purchases, sales, transfers and return to vendors. Of course, you then multiply out the unit stock amount by the retail price to know the retail dollar amount. Again, you have control of your inventory.

So far we have discussed tracking your sales only. Perpetual Inventory gives you an idea of what it is like to follow the total movement of your stock. This helps with analyzing best-selling price points, seasonal assortments, seasonal price points and optimum assortments for groups or basics.

First, we must look at using tickets and labels on items and more about the sales slip. The other components of your inventory management system will follow.

Marking Merchandise and Sales Slips

Most goods need a ticket attached to the item itself. You have seen these mainly on clothing and similar types of items. If your merchandise lends itself to this type of marking, the use of a two-part or three-part ticket serves as the source of sales information. There are also two-part labels available for other types of goods.

Sales staff remove one part of the ticket at the time of the sale and place it in a container. At any time of the day, looking at the tickets is a quick indicator of the day's business. Glancing at the coded information gives you a "feel" for what customers are buying that day.

Use these ticket stubs for the recording of information on the tally sheets and/or perpetual inventory tracking sheets instead of using the sales slips. If sales slips are your primary means of collecting data, make sales staff accountable for the whereabouts of sales slips.

You keep track of the books issued to salespeople by the numbers on the book and telling them not to tear pages out of their books. The books are purchased at an office supply store. If you print your own sales slips and keep track of them, instruct staff that no sales slips are to be discarded. Rather, void and bundle them together with all the sales slips for the day. This gives you some type of control procedure.

When you use an ECR, this is not as crucial. You will move into more sophisticated forms of checks and balances that markedly increase your control.

Much information can be written on a ticket or label. Marking guns allow you to print the information directly onto a label. All information already covered, of course, will go on a ticket or label: department code, subclass, vendor name or code number, and the retail price. You can also put other valuable information on the tickets or labels, including the:

- date put into stock
- size
- color code
- season code

This information is put into code form. Some retailers use the code information as part of their individual stock number. These retailers are tracking the items themselves. If you're only tracking your sales by department and subclass there are valid reasons for wanting to know the above information. The following examples demonstrate common retail situations to emphasize this point:

- You need to take an initial markdown as it is the beginning of the downturn of the season. You select the guidelines of your markdown by the above data on the ticket/label, such as a date that indicates the oldest goods in stock (early receipts for the season) and certain color codes. With these parameters for your markdowns by department, your staff can go to the shelves and racks to find those items without difficulty.

- A vendor has granted you a return label for an item in a particular color. The rep said the color was "hot" (selling extremely well). It sat on your shelves, but the vendor has a customer that will take it all. Your staff pulls out that vendor's goods with that color code. A description of the item also guides them if you don't use your own stock number. If you have placed the date received or date put into stock on the ticket, you have a great qualifier for pulling the goods off the floor fast. (That date can be found on the purchase journal, packing slips, invoices and such.)

Your perpetual inventory sheet shows how many of an item are in stock at a glance.

Use codes that are essential only for your business. Think about what is truly beneficial before getting carried away with lots of codes and numbers. You need information that helps control your inventory. Otherwise, you probably don't need it.

THE PERPETUAL INVENTORY TRACKING FORM

Your goal is to know how many of an item you have in stock. Why do you want to know this? To manage your inventory, you need to make decisions based on these facts to satisfy your customer's needs and wants. Looking at what has been sold or not sold of an item will indicate the direction or action you want to take.

You learn other things from this form as well, such as the response by customers to assortment, color information (if you give each color of an item its own number), vendor response to your reorders and so on.

Store owners who track mainly by department and subclass benefit from using this form for basic items or an item that indicates a future trend. Those using an ECR can program a PLU (Price Look Up number) for the item. You pull a PLU report out of the machine weekly for the data to be entered onto the form. (Each machine will have instructions on the various reports that can be produced from the sales entered into the machine.) The key is to find the combination of tracking formats to obtain the information important to your store and your customer. In managing your inventory, remember that the customer is your reason for being.

Recording on the Perpetual Inventory Form

These are the transactions you will record on this form, in units:

BOM

Sales

Transfers and/or Returns to Vendors

Reorders placed

Totals calculated from the above data yield the next month's BOM. To do this, follow these five steps:

1. The beginning inventory is entered for each item to be tracked. There is a place to enter the name and code number of the department at the top of the form. Don't mix data from different departments. An existing store will do a physical inventory when first instituting the use of this form. A start-up or existing store will enter the number of pieces of a new item when it is received from the vendor at the store.

2. The total from the Quantity Sold column on your Daily Tally Sheet is entered appropriately.

3. Transfers or returns to the vendor are recorded appropriately.

4. Reorders of an item placed with the vendor are entered appropriately under "OO" (On Order).

5. Totals are calculated from these figures monthly telling you exactly how many of the items are in stock starting the next month's business.

PERPETUAL INVENTORY SHEET

DEPARTMENT 05 *Ceramics*   SUBCLASS 42- **Vases** MONTH *Jan.*

Stock #	Description & Vendor Name	Vendor STK #	Retail $	CST $	BOM	WK 1	WK 2	WK 3	WK 4	WK 5	TOT $	EOM	OO
43588	Divine – blue/wht porcelain bud	A 62	18.—	9.—	12	3	2	3	18 1	4	234.—	17	1/15 18pcs

Guideline for Entering Inventory Figures

Goods, when received, are entered in the upper portion of the box for the current week and outgoing goods, like sales and returns, are entered in the lower portion.

This flow of goods is familiar to you since you have calculated the ending and beginning inventories in your OTB plans. Here you are looking at individual items. This gives you a good sense of inventory moving through the store and how it continually does this—with your expert guidance, of course!

A note about another way to follow Perpetual Inventory you may come across from other retailers. Some store owners record an item as it is received. They record all the details of color, size or whatever by the number of each identifier received.

For example: Six pieces of a shirt are received in the store, sized small, medium and large. In the assortment are the following: one small in blue, one small in black; one medium in blue, two mediums in black; one large in black. The blue amount would be recorded on a line and the black on another line, sometimes as hash marks on a style sheet or other form. As each one is sold, a hash mark is crossed out, or a line is drawn through the number and the amount left is entered next to it. **The color of the garment is being used as the identifier for selling trends.**

Personally, I find all of the hash marks difficult to look at and there are too many ways to mess it up. Sure, all those lines crossing out other lines give you a feeling of sales movement. I simply prefer forms to be simple and easy to read. Using an ECR and programming PLUs simplifies this process further.

Using the Perpetual Inventory Form to Evaluate Price Changes

The form included in this book provides quick comparison of amount sold to amount you received. When you record the price change on the line, you are able to determine the effect of a markdown (or markon) on the item. Sales occurring after the price change are directly to the right of the price change. Let's say that you took a "deep" markdown on a slow-moving item early in the season. You felt it was too risky to hold onto it through the season. The week's tally from your Daily Tally Sheet or PLU report entered after the price change shows you immediately the results of your decision.

Use different ink colors for different forms of movement. For example, use blue for receipt of goods, red for the sales and green for transfers and returns to vendors.

Review the sample form that is already filled out. Walk through the calculations yourself and check your answers against those on the form. Play with this for a while.

The perpetual inventory form shows units instead of dollars. Obviously, this is easy to multiply out. Whenever you reorder, calculate the dollars and subtract the amount from the available OTB.

Flow of Merchandise and Your System

Imagine all the components of your stock moving, flowing through your store from the most minute level—each individual item—up through the subclass and then the department, to the total store level. Key your understanding into the need for looking for answers at these various levels. In them lie answers that assist you in controlling your inventory. The forms provided make up the structure of your Inventory Management system.

You will combine the forms to create your own system. Stay flexible and keep your system flexible. As your store grows and changes along with your target market, you'll need to adjust your tracking system. The Sales and Purchase Performance Report (SPPR) will not ever change.

The essential information in the SPPR is just that. Its components are the basis of the Retail Inventory Method, just as there are accounting principles and practices that will not change. This is the same merchandising structure used in computer programs written for retailers.

Keeping Track of Purchases, Returns and on Order Amounts: The Purchase Journal

Recording Purchases as They're Received

The next form is self-explanatory. It accounts for all the information you need to know about goods received. Record your purchase receipts continually. As you evaluate store sales by total store and each department, you must stay on top of the inventory movement in line with the projected beginning inventory of the coming month. You don't want to be overbought.

If you are not tracking individual items, you can skip using the column headed "Stock Number and Description." Enter the total cost and total retail dollar amounts received for that department and subclass. I recommend entering the total number of pieces received in an order to evaluate stock assortments.

Why? When projecting next year's assortment of goods you want to consider the dollar amount and the number of units you had on the racks and shelves. Inflation can affect this total. Sales dollars may increase over the previous year, but is the increase enough to keep you ahead of the inflation rate? Costs on certain types of items may rise or fall due to a change in the manufacturing process. Will you sell as many or more units depending on the change? Perhaps the customer's buying habits are changing based on the number of units they purchase, but the dollar amount they are willing to pay has also changed.

Use your quantity figure to help you with planning of future buys and calculating future OTB plans. This figure relates to your average unit sale in indicating customer buying habits.

PURCHASES RECEIVED AND RETURNS TO VENDOR RECORD

DEPARTMENT_____SUBCLASS_____ MONTH____

P.O. #	Vendor Name	Date Recd.	Comp Date	Stock # and Description	#OF PCS	Cost EA.	Retail. EA.	TOT. Cost	TOT. Retail

To save time and effort in computing the totals for each department, add up the amount ordered for each department on your purchase order copy. You're already working on the quantity to purchase against your OTB so it makes sense to do it only once and be done with it. At the same time you could enter these departmental totals on the Open Order Record, which we will cover next.

Needing the information doesn't mean sitting in your office with papers all the time. Set up notebooks for each form and report that you use and keep them all near one another within easy reach of your work area.

Let's consider the pertinent information needs for a moment. Since the OTB is your control figure, purchases received in any department cannot exceed that dollar figure (at retail, of course). Remember, a good plan is flexible.

Sales may prove higher than expected. Review open (not received as of yet) orders for the current month. Call those vendors and request early delivery if the goods have not already left their distribution center. Buying more merchandise is not always the answer. One department may be much stronger over the others. Overstocking can occur if sales are not as strong throughout the store.

Continually check merchandise received against on order amounts to make decisions quickly in a positive direction rather than simply reacting. You are the guiding force for your store. Deal from a position of strength.

Recording Returns to Vendors

At the bottom of the Purchases Received form is a section for RTVs or Returns to Vendors. Sales is one way merchandise will leave the store. From time to time, however, goods don't live up to the quality the manufacturer showed you in the showroom.

No matter what quality level you set up for your store image and target customer, you don't want merchandise that does not meet that quality. The best avenue in this situation is to get the vendor to give you a return authorization and get it out of your store. This may not be an easy task with some vendors, especially if you are fairly new and have paid up front or COD for goods. Find a recourse with the manufacturer. Consider refusing any other goods from their company if they come in totally different from what was shown to you.

Notice that the headings on the form are slightly different than those for Purchases Received.

RETURN TO VENDOR RECORD										
INVC. #	VENDOR.	REC'D	AUTH #	ITEM# & DESCRIP.	QTY.	COST	RETAIL.	T.CST	T.RTL	COMMENTS
4732	Top Hat	2/10	0704	#515-6" cut crystal flute	2	8 50	17 50	17.—	35.—	Wrong style

First, the invoice number is recorded. You have been billed for the goods and will be issued a credit for the goods returned if no exchange is involved. The fourth column heading is "Auth. #." This abbreviation indicates the Return Authorization sticker number the vendor will supply. The return authorization allows the shipment to receive the proper treatment back at the vendor's plant. Not using one delays the credit due your store. The balance of headings are self-explanatory. Under "Comments" you may want to record the day UPS or other carrier picked up the return shipment. Use it as you find most appropriate for your business.

When goods are returned they appear as an adjustment to the total amount of goods received for the month. Add up all the purchases received for the month in each department/subclass. Then add up any returns and subtract that amount from the total purchases received. The resulting figure at the end of the month is entered in the row designated for "Purchases Received" under the "Actual" column on your Sales and Purchase Performance Report. Later, the RTVs and purchase received are listed separately on the Sales and Purchase Performance Report.

Open Orders

Review any goods not yet received as the completion date nears. Weekly, you calculate sales, purchases received, markdowns and place orders for future times. Goods sell, move out of the store, and new goods come in to replace that stock.

As was presented in Chapter 2 on the Purchase Order and Purchasing System, you will keep a file of open orders for the current month and future delivery dates. Use the Open Order Record to enter and tally up the retail amount of goods to come in by the end of the month for each department and/or subclass. Enter your total dollar figure in pencil. Eliminate the need to re-enter and re-total the same information on a new sheet every time goods come into the store. Rather than just putting an "X" or some other mark next to the entry to prevent addition mistakes, draw a line through the order entry. Total those orders not crossed out. Erase the previous total and enter your new figure.

Look at your Sales and Purchase Performance Report or merchandising plan for the department you are working on. Find the amount of OTB projected. Are you in line? What about the trend in sales for the amount of time passed in the month? The forms are your merchandising tools, not just something to fill out.

				OPEN ORDER RECORD						
DEPARTMENT *Small Decor - 07*							MONTH *MAY*			
P.O. #	Vendor Name	Ship Date	Comp Date	Stock # and Description	#OF PCS	Cost EA.	RTL. EA.	TOT. Cost	TOT. RTL.
0100-42	Sheen	5/25	5/31	total order	32			496.⁻	1,015.⁻
0100-49	Bombay	5/25	5/31	# 107 brass hooks-asst	24	3²⁵	6⁷⁵	78.⁻	162.⁻

USING INVENTORY INFORMATION TO EVALUATE VENDORS

OK. Your store's goods are moving in and out. You're selling merchandise and receiving new merchandise. Another evaluation tool to better your business through your buying relates to your vendors. The next element in Inventory Management is the tracking of price changes. You need to know your vendors more fully through their performance for your store—not just through the designs and fun times in the showroom.

With the two tracking forms we have just worked on, you have the information you need to evaluate each vendor. Recap it every quarter. Certainly before going to market you need to recap for all the vendors with whom you have appointments. Negotiations are easier with the right facts. Price change affects the vendor performance evaluation. Usually, we are talking about markdowns of merchandise not moving (selling) fast enough.

On the Price Change Record, the vendor is recorded along with other information. A vendor with many markdowns in a quarter just is not performing for you. Reasons may include that season's line, the selections recommended by the rep or the styles you bought even though the rep said other stores were not buying them. We do learn from our mistakes!

Evaluate your vendors in the following areas:

- Markon before and after markdowns
- Markdowns
- On-time delivery
- Amount of returns
- Problems with partial shipments
- Total volume of business with each vendor

Consider as well intangible areas that concern vendor performance:

- Customer service
- Flexibility in order changes
- Ease of working with rep
- Trend information shared with you
- Promptness in sending return authorizations

Price Change Record

It would certainly be a perfect world if goods always sold in a timely manner and always at the full retail price. Well, there are many things wonderful about our world, but not every piece of merchandise you buy will sell at the price you set at the initial markon. This is one of the main reasons you have purchased this book—to better your odds by controlling and managing your inventory in the best possible manner and reduce the problems that cut into your profits.

PRICE CHANGES—MARKDOWNS & MARKONS

Markdown: ___X___   Temporary?_____   Permanent?____X____

Department _Small Decor - 07_

Markup:____   DATE TAKEN: ___6/18___

Name/# Vendor	Hash Count	Code # /Sub.	Product Description	Orig Rtl.	Mrkdwn $	Mrkup $	Diff +/-	Total Diff.	Comment
Greenly	////	57	9" red pillow	19.50	15.—		4.50	18—	put on close out table
Greenly	//	51	lace runner	47—	39—		8—	16—	
Sheen	//// /	52	clay pot w/st violet	7—	5—		2—	12—	

There are times when it is necessary to mark down merchandise. Markdowns aren't the only price change options. Here are some scenarios of price adjustments to consider:

Promotional goods purchased that you advertised when the goods first hit the store. The promotional price was printed on the initial ticket. The promotion is over, but the season is still in its early stages. You choose to take a larger markon on the merchandise (within reason so as to be compatible with comparable goods) and integrate the balance of the item into your inventory. Make new tickets with the new, higher retail price.

A private sale will run for selected clientele one evening. Only those items are tagged for the sale. This constitutes a temporary markdown for those items. After the event, pull them back out of stock, recount and ticket with the original retail price. You could use the discount key on the ECR, but your retail dollar amount of the physical inventory would get thrown off without reducing the inventory's retail value. If your ECR reports gross sales by department before and after discounts, your problem is solved. Other options include using a separate tally sheet for the evening or closing out the register before the event in order to use the reading at the end of the evening for your records along with tickets off the merchandise to give you a markdown dollar figure, (the difference between the total original retail on the tickets and the register reading).

A price increase notice is received affecting a basic stock item you carry. The colors are nonseasonal, allowing for new goods at the new price to work into your current stock without any problems. Integrate reorders by re-ticketing all in-stock inventory of the item with the new retail based on marking up the new cost. Yes, you now get a larger markon on those goods you already own. You also just increased the retail dollar amount of your inventory. This points out the need for flexibility in your plan and not placing orders right up to your projected OTB figure.

There are many situations in which you need to make such merchandising decisions. Knowing exactly what happens in your inventory makes this process easier. I can't predict all of them for you—you wouldn't read any book for that long—but you now have the guidelines for handling this decision-making process.

Using the Price Change Record allows you to work on your inventory management at your convenience. Delegate the physical price change work to your sales staff. As you review each month on your Sales and Purchase Performance Report, make the necessary decisions on markdowns to move goods out of the store.

Taking a markdown isn't bad. Marking goods down in a timely fashion exemplifies good money control. Be smart and get your money out of an item before the markdown will have little effect. Old goods don't move well at any price. Reinvesting the money in the areas that show strong sales makes more sense.

Recording Transfers

It is not too soon to think about transfers even if you have only one store. Transfers aren't always between different units of a chain. A transfer is an adjustment affecting ending physical inventory. For instance:

- a department becomes too large and is divided into two or more new departments providing more concise trend information;

- a department becomes obsolete and another department absorbs the merchandise;

- merchandise is expensed out when used as a giveaway in a promotion or donation to a charity;

- an item is expensed out as a display item and not marked for resale.

An actual form isn't necessary for a one-store operation, but recording the transfer is important. I recommend adding a divider to the notebook used for your purchase and RTV journal records for transfers. If you are changing departments and merchandise around a lot, then rethink your department classifications. Something is amiss.

Look closely at the amount of merchandise moved into or out of a department. Count it as it is re-tagged. This is like taking a spot inventory to check for shrinkage. Proper calculation of the existing inventory supports your inventory management system, where assuming the book inventory to be the transferred amount would not.

Those using some form of perpetual inventory form or stock card need to record transfers of merchandise here as well for those items affected.

In the event you do have more than one store, then the transfer from one store should be treated as a purchase by the receiving store. Transferring goods from one store to another can reduce inventory costs. This is an excellent tactic to cut down on special orders from vendors and reduce the cost of carrying added inventory. The flexibility in your OTB plans and not buying up to your projected OTB allow this transfer buy.

RECAP OF INVENTORY MANAGEMENT SYSTEM

Components of your inventory movement

- Recording of sales

- Tracking of incoming and outgoing inventory through purchases and returns to vendors

- Recording and calculation of price changes

- Recording of merchandise transfers
- Maintaining perpetual inventory on specific items
- Vendor recap for evaluation

These basic components of your inventory management system provide the tools with which you investigate possibilities in merchandising and create your own road and direction.

By now you see how these components come together into the Sales and Purchase Performance Report. Let's look further into Inventory Management before we move on. Then we will look at Financial Control to talk about areas not directly related to inventory and a few that do relate; Merchandising Techniques, the physical store layout and visual impact you can create with your merchandise; Buying Strategies, how you will work with the tools calculated here to manage the inventory better and create more profits.

SALES AND PURCHASE PERFORMANCE REPORT DEPARTMENT/TOTAL STORE

Month/ Oct.   Month/ Nov.   Month/ Dec.

Prev. EOM   71,200

	L.Y.	Plan	Actual	L.Y.	Plan	Actual	L.Y.	Plan	Actual
S/S Ratio	3.40	3.75	3.75	3.20	2.80	2.84	2.80	1.70	1.72
Sales	16,900	19,000	19,012	23,700	26,000	25,687	40,980	45,000	43,475
% Inc.<Dec>		12.0	12.49		8.80	8.34		9.0	6.08
Plan MDs									
Revised Plan									
BOM (@ Retail)		71,250	71,200		72,800	73,078		76,500	74,794
Revised Plan									
On Order									
Open To Buy		10,550			29,700			28,500	
Purc.Recd.			20,890			27,403			29,000
MDs Taken									
Revised OTB									

Recap for Period   Remarks

avg. stock
69,847.75

	Cost	Retail	avg.initial markon % 51.26
1. Net purchases	37,675	77,293	
2. Stock on Hand @ beg of period		71,200	
3. Total Mdse Handled		148,493	annual turn
4. Net Sales		88,174	5.05
5. Markdowns			
6. Markons		Dept:_____	
7. Out of Stocks		%of total	store total
8. Shrinkage		Mo.1	19,012
9. Total adjustments		Mo.2	25,687
10. Ending Inv. @ end of period		Mo.3	43,475
		60,319	

BRINGING IT ALL TOGETHER

The Sales and Purchase Performance Report

Take a long, close look at the SPPR. Note all the components we have just discussed. There are also additional items with new formulas for you to work with:

- average initial markon
- annual turn, projected
- average stock
- computing ending inventory/BOM for the next month
- making the adjustments to the inventory

The SPPR gives a total picture of each department's health and trends. When you put together a SPPR for the total store, you know easily where to troubleshoot.

We'll take a walk through the report first and then address some of the new formulas mentioned above.

Three months appear on a report. Do an SPPR for each department. Looking at the figures in the SPPR for each month you know if:

1. Sales are up or down.
2. Inventory is in line with plan.
3. Markdowns are heavier or lighter than planned.
4. The S/S Ratio is in line with plan.
5. You are over or under bought.

A note about the last point. I continually emphasize the need to never buy up to the total OTB figure. Recording purchases and sales weekly quickly clues you in to trouble areas. Are sales and/or purchases out of line with plan? At that point, most likely mid-month, you adjust incoming orders. I'll discuss how to do this in Chapter 6, Buying Strategies.

Sales and BOM

Each department has a total sales figure tallied from the various forms you choose—one of the daily tally sheets and/or the perpetual inventory form. Use these figures to fill out a SPPR for the department or sales store when added together. Calculate your sales as follows:

1. Enter each department's sales under the actual column on the SPPR.
2. Then, total all departments' sales for the total store SPPR.

3. Net Sales in the recap at the bottom of the report is the total of all the months on the report. Two months calculated would be added together or three months to fill out the SPPR fully .

BOM

Take inventory when you implement the use of a formal inventory management system. A new store has all of these figures available from purchase orders and purchase receipt journals. This gives you the first month's BOM, which is also the "Prev. EOM." If you start mid-month, make a note for yourself somewhere on the report in order to use that information properly in next year's planning.

That takes care of the very first month's BOM. What about as you continue through this report and onto others?

Figuring the BOM for the Next Month

Enter all your plan figures from your OTB plan under the plan column for each month. The lines to use are:

> S/S RATIO
> SALE
> % INC. <DEC.>
> PLAN MD'S
> BOM @ RETAIL
> Open to Buy

Use this as a checklist while you get used to the form.

Now you must also enter the actual data to compare your plan to the actual figures. The checklist for these follows:

- Purchases received
- Sales
- Markdowns taken
- Shrinkage or other adjustments

These components resemble those in the OTB formula. The OTB is now in the form of actual Purchases Received.

$$BOM + PURCHASES - REDUCTIONS = EOM$$

Of course, that EOM is the next month's BOM!

Inventory is reduced by:

> SALES
>
> MARKDOWNS
>
> SHRINKAGE ADJUSTMENTS
>
> ANY OTHER ADJUSTMENTS FOR OUT OF STOCK

Use your calculator to work with the figures in the example.

Notice that when all three months have occurred, the last "Physical Inv. @ end of period" on line 10 of the recap is a figure not anywhere else on the SPPR. How right you are! That is the next month's BOM on the next SPPR!

Note: one other component of the recap—purchases are recorded at cost and retail.

The Recap of all Periods in the SPPR

At the bottom is a recap of all months in the report. Since many stores look at the year broken up into seasons, this is a pertinent way to look at your store for a period of time.

As each month of figures occurs, the previous totals have that month's totals added to them. The only figure that will not have any changes made to it is on line 2 in the recap, "Stock on Hand @ beg of period." This figure is the same as the "Prev. EOM" and the "BOM @ RETAIL" on the SPPR.

Now, let's calculate the trend information and evaluation tools in the Sales and Purchase Performance Report.

Figuring the Stock to Sales Ratio

This is quite easy, since you already know that sales multiplied by a S/S Ratio produce a beginning inventory.

Thus:

> BOM ÷ SALES = S/S RATIO

Figuring the Average Markon

All purchases received during the period are added together. Each month, take these totals of cost and retail to figure the markon.

> (TOTAL RETAIL - TOTAL COST) ÷ TOTAL RETAIL

Just as in any other markon calculation, this determines the markon percentage. You've worked hard at selecting your goods and planning the inventory levels. You want to make sure you didn't miss anything in planning your markon goals for incoming goods.

Figuring Average Stock @ Retail

Remember figuring the average stock from using the sales and stockturn figures in planning? To monitor this and get a different perspective on the inventory level, you figure average stock carried.

Divide by the number of figures added together. You always have one more figure than the number of months you are adding.

# of months divide by:

One month of sales 2

Two months of sales 3

Three months of sales 4

Why? You add the beginning inventory for every month in the equation as well as the ending inventory. This presents the extra figure.

Example: Two months in the report

(Mo.1 BOM + Mo.2 BOM + EOM) ÷ 3 = Average Stock

One month in the report

(Mo.1 BOM + EOM) ÷ 2 = Average Stock

Use your calculator to figure the same from the example SPPR. Add together all of the actual "BOM @ RETAIL" figures and the Ending Inventory, then divide by four to arrive at the Average Stock @ Retail.

Figuring Annual Turn

Total Sales ÷ Average Stock

Now, you ask, what if I only have one month on the report? Multiply the resulting figure of the above by 12.

Then:

2 months, multiply by 6

3 months, multiply by 4

This gives you the ANNUAL TURN rate for the sales and inventory trend at present. If you are not coming close to plan, then corrective steps need to be taken.

Figuring Department Contribution

Here, all we want to know is what size of the total pie this piece is. Just as you would figure any other percentage in relation to another figure divide the department sales by the total store sales.

Total Dept. Sales ÷ Total Store Sales = % of Store

MAKING ADJUSTMENTS TO THE INVENTORY

In the recap section of the SPPR, there is a line for shrinkage. As a reduction of inventory, you cannot know how much shrinkage you have without taking a physical inventory. Only then will you know the difference between what is actually in stock and what you should have in stock.

Just like the OTB, the total ending inventory figure for the period is a control figure for maintaining a certain level of inventory. It is the book inventory. You tracked all the goods coming in and going out of your store. You tracked any changes to that inventory through recording the markdowns, markons and other adjustments, plus the sales. The book inventory is what should be in the store.

Taking Physical Inventory

Most retailers take an inventory and adjust the book inventory twice a year. This is a sound practice to follow. The line titled "Shrinkage" is for this purpose on the SPPR. You may feel there is something wrong in the store and that you are losing merchandise. Take a spot inventory in any department and check that figure against your book figure. Scrutinize any discrepancies that appear out of line. Spot check your paperwork. Unfortunately, if shortages appear you probably need to look at what you and your staff are doing to discourage theft in the store.

How to Make the Adjustment

Adjust the inventory in the recap portion of the SPPR by deducting the amount from "Merchandise Handled." If you are at the end of a period then deduct the difference from the book inventory, "Physical Inv. at End of Period," with the resulting figure used as the BOM figure to start the new SPPR.

Be sure you have your accountant adjust your inventory on your balance sheet (carried at cost) as well. Using the profit and loss statement, you can figure the percentage that will be closest to your cumulative markon. In this case, it will be the cost of goods sold without the freight cost. Without using a computer to track every item in and out of the store at cost and retail, you can't have an exact cost figure.

However, this works very well for independents to adjust the cost value of their inventory. Using the initial markon would not reflect the cost of the goods since at any time of the year you will have markdown goods in the store.

ACTION LIST FOR CHAPTER 3

• Decide how you want to mark stock. Use an item code and department/subclass, with vendor code or item code and vendor number or other system that you choose.

• Select a tally sheet or the perpetual inventory form to track sales.

• Select the ticketing form for your various types of goods, stickers or tags.

• Set up Purchase Received Journal sheets for each department.

• New stores about to open need to tally up purchases received to know their beginning inventory.

• Existing stores need to take inventory to learn BOM totals for each department, subclass and total store. (You may need to re-ticket merchandise first if you have changed department designations, etc.)

• List open orders from your Open Order files. Check figures against your OTB plans to spot needed cancellations or increases. (See Chapter 6 for buying strategies.)

• Copy the Sales and Purchase Performance Report form (in Appendix III) to do monthly analysis (preparing for Chapter 6, Buying Strategies).

• Record historical data into SPPR for each quarter to be reviewed. (Tip: Do a quarter such as May, June, July, then start another with July, August, September to provide more continuity and better buying.)

Chapter 4

Financial Control

The goals of the business support your overall personal goals and why you are doing what you are doing—namely, why you are in business.

YOUR MOTIVATION

1. Survival and growth of the business.
2. Desire for a profitable return on your investment.
3. Serve the community.
4. Social recognition and status.

Look closely at these, because 1, 3 and 4 certainly won't happen without the positive results of number 2.

Growth requires profit for reinvestment.

To spur growth, we seek ways to increase volume and profits. In this chapter, we investigate the operational viewpoint and necessary functions within the business. Factors affecting this include:

1. Sales volume

2. Cost of goods (merchandise) sold (COGS)

3. Operating expenses

4. Other income

PROFIT AND LOSS STATEMENT

Many terms are contained in the Income Statement, or Profit and Loss Statement. This financial statement provides you with the operational viewpoint. Words describe it well enough, but let's take a pictorial look at the Profit and Loss Statement's main components.

	1. SALES $
–	2. COGS $
	GROSS PROFIT $
–	3. OPERATING EXPENSES $
	OPERATING PROFIT $
+	4. NET OTHER INCOME $
	NET PROFIT BEFORE TAXES $

Or, in other words:

Sales minus Cost of Goods Sold = Gross Profit

Gross Profit minus Operating Expenses = Operating Profit

Operating Profit plus Net Other Income = Net Profit Before Taxes

Most people feel that they do not have control over Cost of Goods Sold so they look at the Income Statement from the Gross Profit down. However, as you have learned in planning out OTB, you can have control. For example, with astute buying practices you can obtain goods at lower prices from your suppliers. Other methods include:

- Improvement of the merchandise mix reducing COGS in relation to Sales
- Careful inventory control reduces the extent to which the value of your inventory depreciates
- Decrease the average inventory or increase sales with the same average inventory

Here are terms relating to the profit perspective of your business and the income statement in more detail:

Operating Statement, P&L, Income Statement: The financial statement that depicts the profit overview encompassing operating expenses. Operating expenses include all costs related to the selling of goods over and above the actual purchases themselves.

Profit: What we all hope to make in our businesses. This is not so much a term here as a gentle reminder of one of the main reasons we are here doing this together.

Operating Profit: The dollar and percentage amount of profit made from sales after deducting COGS and Operating Expenses.

Net Profit: Profit amount after any additional income is added onto the Operating Profit and deductions relating to the Other Income are subtracted.

Other Income: That income from non store areas, such as interest from a bank account.

Deductions From Other Income: Any costs relating to the Other Income.

Net Other Income: The sum of the two above figures.

Gross Sales: All sales of the store(s) before any adjustments.

Returns and Allowances: The dollar amount of goods returned to the store and any allowances made to customers in order to sell goods. This reduces the Gross Sales figure.

Net Sales: The total sales of the store after employee discounts and returns.

Purchases: The amount of goods purchased for resale in the store.

Total Merchandise Handled: Beginning Inventory plus actual purchases. Most income statements do not show this figure.

Cost Of Goods Sold (COGS): The total cost of goods for any one time period calculated by subtracting End of the Month Inventory from the Total Merchandise Handled and adding in the cost of freight, cleaning, repairing, etc. Any cash discounts would be subtracted from the sum to get a total figure for the COGS.

Gross Margin: Most people don't distinguish this from Gross Profit, but please be advised that GM is the percent figure resulting from Gross Profit divided by the Net Sales. Gross Profit is the dollar figure.

Operating Expenses: All those expenses that are incurred running your store.

Returns To Vendors: Goods returned to the vendor. This reduces the COGS in the period that it occurs.

Allowance From Vendors: Any credits or cash discounts allowed by the vendor. This reduces your COGS.

Promotional Allowance: An allowance specifically credited your store for promotions performed by you.

Consignment Purchases (As Part Of Inventory): Goods not purchased outright by you. Some stores do this with new, small vendors to try them out. Remember that this is inventory in your store and should not be disregarded in relation to your merchandise plan.

Transfer In: Goods brought in from another store in your chain. This is a way to "buy" from yourself and reserve cash.

Transfer Out: Goods moved out of one store to another.

Stock Alterations: Any cost incurred to maintain or alter stock in order to make it saleable or to complete a sale.

Maintained Markon: Net Sales minus Gross COGS (before any adjustments of cash discounts earned and alterations divided by Net Sales.

Chart of Accounts

A term you hear from many sources, including your accountant, is the Chart of Accounts. This is simply the list of every item that pertains to the balance sheet and the income statement. Every item is referred to as an account and each has its own code number for entry into your accountant's computer program (or your own if you are producing your own statements).

A sample chart of accounts that pertains to both financial statements is in Appendix II. You can make yours more or less detailed depending on your preference and the needs of your business for particular types of information.

MARKDOWNS AND THE GROSS MARGIN

In taking a markdown, the inventory has been devalued. With a lower selling price, you have a lower net sales in relation to the cost of goods sold. Thus, the gross margin shrinks with increased markdowns.

This is why it is so important to plan the dollar amount and percentage of markdowns for your store. Compare your figures to others in the industry. The better your buying becomes through using the OTB plan, markdowns decrease by being on target much more often.

Other factors affecting your gross margin are:

- Shrinkage
- Discounts

These reduce the inventory value and net sales, reducing turn and your profit margin. Review the Inventory Management chapter as often as needed to understand fully how this interacts with the other components in the SPPR.

TERMS AND DATING

Along with determining the type of merchandise appropriate for your store to serve the needs of your identified consumer group(s) comes the responsibility of controlling cash. Understand invoicing and dating terms to achieve this goal.

Invoicing Terms and Dating

Initially, many if not most of your vendors will ask you to pay outright before shipment or C.O.D. (Cash On Delivery). Let's look at what marketing students know as Utilities to approach the importance of this side of financial control. This depicts the flow of the business itself and the interaction of various functions.

Form Utility: Understanding your target market in terms of product components (color, style, size, price and quality) based on customer life style or other needs, depending on your store concept.

Place Utility: Stocking the merchandise in the store to make it convenient for the customer to locate and create a retail environment consistent with the psychographics and taste level.

Time Utility: Having goods available when the customer wants to purchase them.

Possession Utility: Offering the necessary forms of transactions—Cash, Credit, etc.—along with service consistent with the needs of the customer—Delivery, Alterations, Layaway.

As a buyer, you are responsible for understanding your target market's wants and needs. You then interpret those into goods, those items of merchandise that will satisfy the first three utilities, form, place and time.

These are very practical points to assist you in understanding that where, how and when customers get merchandise affects the financial stature of your store.

You switch hats to make the decisions to satisfy the fourth utility, Possession. As an owner of an independent store, you find that distinct lines between jobs exist only in semantics. While wearing your buyer's hat, you seek out vendors and other resources to satisfy your concept and target market. How long your resources allow before payment is due is part of this decision. You want to control your available (and soon-to-be available) funds since it takes time to sell goods.

Ask the resource—"What are your terms and dating?"

Every industry has its own terms, which you'll find consistent throughout the industry. Chalk up your first few trips to market as learning experiences. You'll quickly learn the terms and dating nuances. How you use them to control your cash and know where you stand at any point in time financially is more important.

The Components of Terms

Terms contain three components. Here are the names and descriptions of those terms:

1. & 2. An allowed discount deduction if you pay on or before a specified amount of time. This is the **Cash Discount** and appears like this—2/10—

when written on the invoice. The slash separates the percentage (the first figure) from the number of days allowed to take the discount (the second figure). The first component is the allowed deduction, and the second the amount of time in which the deduction is allowed to be taken.

3. The last date payment must be made, which is without the discount deduction allowance. This number is preceded with either an "N" or the word "Net."

NOTE: When you set up your chart of accounts for your business, remember that "discounts and allowances" should appear under the "Cost of Goods Sold." This allows you to evaluate your usage of these tools in your business. If you separate them, you know exactly how much you take in cash discounts and other allowances off the cost prices of goods.

Example of terms and dating:

8/10 Net 30

> 8% discount allowed in 10 days from date of the invoice or the net amount due in 30 days.

5/15 N20

> 5% discount allowed in 15 days or Net due in 20 days.

Take cash discounts. Your cash can't earn enough to offset it. Here is what I mean—the following chart shows the percent of annualized cost of credit if you did not take the discount:

Credit Terms	%
1/10 net 20	36.36%
1/10 net 30	18.18%
2/10 net 20	73.44%
2/10 net 30	36.72%

You save more than just the dollar amount of the cash discount when you take it. Large stores fight diligently for terms from their vendors. Borrowing money is almost always cheaper unless interest rates go very high.

PREPARING FINANCIAL STATEMENTS

Retailers write a lot of checks and have lots of expenditures to track. Until you feel comfortable with the statements and grow enough to handle this administrative function, use an accountant. Running your store in all the merchandising aspects is more than a full-time job. Learning about financial statements and the nitty-gritty of debits and credits could send you up the wall fast.

CHOOSING AN ACCOUNTANT

Spend plenty of time searching out an accountant. Referrals from friends only give you a start at finding one. Interview candidates to find someone with whom you will feel comfortable. Ask questions about what they think is best for your business. Compare the answers of each and weigh them carefully. Educate yourself about financial statements and other accounting facets of your business structure. This better prepares you to understand the answers to your questions.There are different structures of businesses:

> Sole Proprietorship
>
> Partnership
>
> Corporation—"S" or "C" election

They have different tax advantages and disadvantages.

You will be asking a lot of questions relating to income taxes as your business grows. Obtain legal advice to choose the business structure best for your store and your personal financial position. Both areas need to be considered in choosing the business structure. Unfortunately or fortunately, the legal issue of liability can outweigh other cost-saving considerations to protect your personal assets. Your individual situation needs to be considered to determine the legal and tax advantages and disadvantages of each particular business structure.

IN-STORE ACCOUNTING

Here, we will cover journals you keep to provide current information. When you send your financial data out to an accountant, you probably won't see your statements for three weeks. Those statements present the historical picture of the total operation. As you have already learned, retail inventory method will key you current with daily and weekly data needed to take action as quickly as possible. But you also need an operational viewpoint using financial statements.

Run your business—don't let it run you.

Let's look at the necessary components of financial control:

- Income Summary
- Purchase Journal
- Asset Journal

Other financial controls you need are:

- Tracking Layaways
- Daily Deposit Reconciliation
- Cash Flow Projections

Some of these, like tracking layaways or the purchase journal, look like merchandising and inventory control pieces. They work with the tracking needed for your SPPR.

We have already looked at a capsule view of the P & L in the beginning of this chapter. Let's look closer at it now. The P & L is a record of the results over a period of time (usually a month or a quarter) of the business's operation. This is where the phrase "bottom line" came from.

First, the INCOME SUMMARY:

INCOME

GROSS SALES

- RETURNS & ALLOWANCES

= NET SALES

Track from your tickets or ECR tapes the returns and allowances (such as discounts). Returns are goods put back into stock for resale. Allowances are discounts given to the customer in some form—either a percentage off the sale or a dollar allowance for a customer willing to take a damaged item or other reason. Imagine how important it is to use these selling tools in your store. The Net Sales is the complement figure when calculating the percent of total for any other expense item. We'll see this as we review Cost of Goods Sold. Always remember that NET SALES is 100 percent on your P & L.

Some cash registers don't track discounts and such. All the more reason to track your markdowns so you at least have some idea of an area that reduces your gross sales.

Your income summary consists of gross sales, returns and allowances in each department. You chart this daily on your daily tally sheets to get your store total. Many components of your inventory system provide you with information needed in other parts of your system.

For example, sales figures go:

- next to your last year's figures in your "To Beat Book"
- on each department's Sales and Purchase Performance Report
- on the income journal for the accountant to produce your financial statements.

The Purchase Journal

We have already worked with this in the Inventory Management section. Here, we want to look at the total cost of inventory in relation to the total store operation. Combine all of the store's purchases for the month. But there are other costs related to purchases.

What did it cost you to bring those goods into the store? Ah! Wise question! Costs to consider:

- Which carrier to use
- Frequency of ordering

Looking at the frequency of your purchases, you realize that incoming freight costs go up. Too many small shipments from a vendor can cause this. If you have not paid attention to items that should have been reordered and now you must pay for a faster rate of delivery, again, the cost goes up. This is why you want to know what percentage of your net sales is in freight costs.

We've discussed taking cash discounts. The purchase journal should show the amount you took in cash discounts and any allowances from the vendor. This will decrease the total amount of your Cost of Goods Sold.

Calculating COGS from the monthly purchase journal:

Inventory purchases	$4,597.00
Freight in	$ 112.00
Cost of purchases	$4,709.00
Less: Discounts	$ 191.94
Total COGS	$4,517.06

Other costs increase the COGS. They include:

- Cleaning of items
- Repair
- Alterations
- Special delivery service costs

The advantage of separating out these costs is to view the percentage of net sales going to these expenses. This gives you the ability to target easily and quickly expenses needing improvement.

CASH BASIS AND ACCRUAL ACCOUNTING

Cash and **Accrual** are two types of accounting methods—how you track and document everything about your operation. You can learn more about accounting through other books and resources, like accountants. (Their fee might be more than you want to spend for an education. Look to them for clarification on your operation and tax advice.)

Cash accounting records transactions just as the money flows. When you are paid, a sale is recorded. The same is true when you pay an invoice. The expense is recorded when the money goes out.

Accrual is a more realistic picture of what condition the business is in when the financial statement is produced. Sales and expenses are recorded as they occur, not when the money comes in or goes out. An invoice for merchandise received is a part of your COGS even though you did not pay it yet. It appears on your balance sheet as an outstanding payable. Of, course you should discuss this with your accountant while you look at your total financial position. You can see a month's operation more clearly with accrual rather than with the ups and downs of cash flow.

According to the IRS and 1986 Tax Reform, businesses with inventory doing under $5 million in sales can choose between the two accounting methods. Businesses above that sales level must use the accrual method. Previous to reform, all stores had to use the accrual method. Neither I nor the accountants I worked with recommended that our clients affected by this change to the cash method.

When the accrual method is done properly, your COGS for a month or quarter is calculated using the beginning and the ending inventory at cost. This means that you can see for that period of accounting the cost of goods to produce that period's sales. Look at the following example of accrual calculation of Cost of Goods Sold:

Calculating Cost of Goods Sold by accrual:

Beginning Inventory	$39,845.00
Purchases	$ 4,597.00
Freight In	$ 112.00
Cost of Purchases	$44,554.00
Disc. & Allowances	$ 191.94
Ending Inventory	$38,772.00
COGS	$ 5,590.06

If you used the cash accounting method, your COGS would only show purchases you paid. Accrual accounting puts the sales and COGS figure in a direct, meaningful relationship. It shows the true cost of the sales that occurred in a month or year-to-date on the financial statement. The same is true of the receivables and payables.

Many more explanations on debits, credits and the keeping of books would assist in this accounting function. Please see the Bibliography for books on this particular subject (p. 123). This knowledge will always be of service to you, even if you do not produce your own financial statements.

As your business grows, at some point you will want to computerize the merchandising functions you have learned here in this book. One of the advantages of this becomes apparent in the accounting recordkeeping of your business. If you purchase an accounting software package with your merchandising software, purchase orders, sales, returns and such are transferred electronically to the accounting software. This greatly reduces the time to enter data, the time collecting the information, not to mention the time spent balancing it all!

The Asset Journal

You have other assets on your balance sheet:

- Leasehold improvements
- Display fixtures
- Items that help you conduct your business like your ECR and possibly a computer.

Record these items as you purchase them. These are not "expensed" off the income in the year they are purchased. If you were building your own financial statements, you would write a check. And, instead of putting the amount (as a debit) onto the expense journal, you'd enter it onto your asset journal. If you use an accountant, this is as simple as indicating it on your check register or making a list of those items. Include the date purchased and purchase price.

Many clients have asked me, "What qualifies as an asset?" There are guidelines for tax purposes that you need to ask your accountant about. When you put together or expand your store, items that are large purchases and fall under one of the above three categories are generally assets. Assets are depreciated over a set period of time relating to the life of the item according to IRS regulations.

If you purchase a store, part of the purchase includes goodwill. This is a nontangible asset that is amortized over a period of time. Depreciation and amortization appear on both the balance sheet and the income statement. They decrease the value of the asset on your balance sheet and show up in (increased) expenses on the income statement.

Why? Most likely, you have borrowed funds to purchase the asset. Borrowed funds are paid back over time. Therefore you do not expense the item immediately but over time as well. The time between each has no relationship.

Depreciation and amortization schedules are guided by IRS regulations. Borrowed funds obviously are subject to the deal made between you and the loan source—bank, friend, venture capital and so on.

DAILY RECONCILIATION

Every day you will have a deposit and that deposit needs to be reconciled against your sales figures. This is a financial control, or what most would call part of the checks and balances within a firm.

You learn more about your business here as well. In reconciling your deposit you see how much of your business is done on bank charge cards, by check or cash. Most businesses average about 30 percent of their sales in bank charge cards. Add up your sales projections and figure the projected amount of credit card purchases. Shop for a bank that offers you a good discount rate for those deposits.

The automatic card reading systems that check the credit are well worth the cost. They save time in writing up deposits and also help reduce your rate paid on those deposits due to reduced paperwork for the bank as well.

There are deposit reconciliation forms. Every accountant has one or more for different clients. I have included in the book a one-page daily reconciliation form. You can condense this to include a full week on one sheet by not separating the components as I have. There are separations between Sales, Register Readings, Deposit Totals and a Balancing formula to allow you the luxury of some space while you get used to doing this. Feel free to adapt it as you please in the future.

Let's look at the deposit reconciliation form sections:

Sales: Your cash register will have gross totals of each of the payment possibilities you program. If returns are separated out on the readout, you can record it here.

Other Register Readings: You need to know how much cash should be in the drawer (the register will calculate this), how many gift certificates sold or redeemed and how much cash came out of the drawer for a petty cash expense. (This last component is also a feature on electronic cash registers.)

You need additional information each month to file your sales tax returns, including shipping fees you collected and the breakdown of taxable and non-taxable goods sold.

Deposit: Add up all the components of your deposit.

To Balance: Your sales data and deposit totals must match to balance. If not, you are either "short" or "long." Short means a deposit smaller than your sales records. Long means the opposite. Below the deposit is the formula for balancing. Notice how gift certificates adjust the Gross Sales depending on whether they were redeemed or sold (purchased by a customer).

DEPOSIT

Cash	$429.36
Checks	$123.79
MC/VISA	$ 89.54
AM.EX.	$257.22
Total Deposit	$899.91

TO BALANCE:

Adjusted Gross Sales	$889.96
+ Gift Certificates Sold	$ 25.00
– Gift Certificates Redeemed	$ 10.00
– Petty Cash	$ 5.00
Deposit Amount	$899.96

This deposit happens to be over (long) by a nickel. There is one very important thing to remember:

THE DRAWER BANK

Whatever amount you choose to keep for your "bank" in the register, you must count it out before doing your deposit. Then you count the rest of the cash that is deposited the next day. Depending on your business, you will keep various ratios of coin and bills to make change. The bank should always be checked well before the store opens to prevent running out of change during the day.

The petty cash journal at the bottom of the form helps when accounting for all expenses at the month end.

TRACKING LAYAWAYS

The layaway is a selling tool you should consider offering. You need to keep a separate notebook of when, who and how much in order to keep the layaway process organized.

Establish a layaway policy and make sure all employees know it well. Use signage if you like to offer or even explain the policy. Remember to have a time limit. Whatever deposit and payments you receive on an item that is never picked up won't help much if the item becomes too old to sell.

Store the item well while payments are being made. Make customers as happy when they pick it up as when they first decided to make the purchase.

Layaways are a receivable and should appear on the asset side of your balance sheet. Keep close tabs on them and keep your records in order. Customers become very frustrated if all their paperwork is not there when they make their final payment. Layaways help increase your sales, so use them to make a loyal customer at the same time.

THE CASH FLOW PROJECTION FORM

Also, in Appendix III is a Cash Flow Projection Form covering six months. Operation Expenses is defined as "all those expenses that are incurred running your store." Merchandise is not an expense in this strict sense.

Review the Six-Month Cash Flow Projections Form in the Appendix. This form is as complete as possible to suit many retailers. If you are a start-up, use this list as a guideline of costs to organize and open your store. Use the first column to list start-up costs. Almost every item on this list will come up in the start-up stages.

Purchases and Inventory: We have covered this on a planning scale. You must plan an opening inventory to present your store when you open. This is the initial BOM on your OTB plan at cost.

Salaries: Payroll doesn't start when you open the doors. All of the inventory you ordered to open the store needs to be checked in, verified to be in good condition, tagged with the proper price and then merchandised on the shelves and racks.

Payroll Taxes: States and localities have varying percentages of taxes that you are responsible for as well as those employees have taken out of their checks. Unemployment tax is one such cost to you and not the employee. As an employer, you match the FICA and Medicaid that is taken out of the employee's salary. Check with your accountant to uncover any other taxes. A much overlooked tax is FUTA, the federal government's unemployment tax. This is usually paid yearly. Regulations about such taxes change, so be sure that your accountant keeps you up-to-date on your payroll responsibilities.

You may consider hiring a service such as Paychex or ADP. These services keep track of your payroll responsibilities for you, sending you forms to sign and indicating the amount you owe to the proper government agency and when to pay. This service pays for itself many times over in time saved. Some services even guarantee your records will be correct or they will pay penalties.

Advertising: This includes marketing and advertising costs. You can separate out print media (newspapers and magazines) from other marketing tools to see this part of your business better. Any communication with your customers is really marketing—signs, banners, radio ads, postcards, list rentals, thank you notes—all of it. Opening your store will include doing many forms of marketing to get the word out.

Bad Check/Debts: It's doubtful you will have any of these before you open unless you do some special showings, previews or shows. Bad checks are those that you cannot collect. Some businesses are more prone to this problem than others. One bookstore owner said, "Book lovers don't write bad checks." In many years of operations she had never had a bad check. A liquor store is most likely a different story.

Subscriptions/Associations: To keep up with your industry and the consumer, you will want to belong to specific associations and subscribe to magazines and papers that keep you informed. Doing this far in advance of opening will sharpen your skills and knowledge of running a store in your field.

Professional Fees: Before opening your store, you will work with an attorney on your lease, incorporation, partnership agreement or other such documents. An accountant you have selected will set up your books and perhaps help you with your cash flow projections.

Freight Out: If you ship for customers or deliver purchases to them this expense is not part of the merchandise cost. If you must do special packaging, it would be helpful for you to keep track of it separately under supplies. A gourmet chocolate store purchased special cold packs to ship truffles all around the country in any weather. Special boxes were also purchased. When you track sales, the shipping charge the customer pays is a part of sales but should be tracked separately. Then you can compare these two figures on the legal P & L instead of digging through invoices, sales slips and register tape.

Office and Postage: You won't believe how much you'll spend in postage just paying bills! Postage that is for marketing should be tracked in Advertising/Marketing. Pens, scratch pads, purchase orders and such are all part of your office expenses.

Rent and Common Area: When you rent a space you will pay deposits. Project these out on the cash flow form. In your financial statements, they are recorded on the balance sheet. Common area usually pertains to an additional dollar amount per square foot if you rent in a mall. You may even have security fees. Before renting a space, be sure you know all of the costs. A dollar figure quoted by a real estate agent is usually just the base rent, and the common area or other fees are quoted separately. Of course, just like anything else, they are negotiable.

Utilities and Telephone: Hook up your phone a couple of weeks or more before opening. You will be there a lot and you may need to talk to your vendors about merchandise that did not come or come in correct quantities, etc.

Employees will need to be called. You will be doing interviews, working with artists or other marketing people for ads, flyers and more. Signs need to be delivered, and workers will be all over the place doing last minute touches to finish your leasehold improvements. Without a telephone, you're out of touch.

Insurance: There are many options when you buy insurance to cover your store. Spend a lot of time understanding what a policy will and will not pay for. If there's a fire next door and you have smoke-damaged merchandise, will it be covered? At what dollar amount—your actual cost or replacement cost? Cost of insurance is greatly affected with the way the building was built and with what type of materials. An option in insurance policies covers lost business if you are closed. This is a very expensive option, and few business owners choose it. Ask for a sample policy. This is a trick an insurance professional taught me. Most agents will be shocked and reluctant to give it to you. Brochures just don't tell you what they really do and don't pay on a claim.

Another type of insurance, key person insurance, relates to you and/or any partners you may have in your business. In the event something happens to you or a partner, this policy helps by injecting cash into the business to replace that person's duties.

If you borrow money through the SBA guarantee loan program, you will have to carry life insurance for the amount of the loan with the SBA as beneficiary. You must have proof of the insurance at closing for your loan, otherwise disbursement of funds will be delayed.

Taxes and Licenses: Every municipality has its own ordinances and regulations. Some states have an inventory tax or personal property tax on the items used in the business, such as computers, office furniture and other depreciable assets. Check with the county and city offices where you are locating the store. A good source of accumulated start-up information is a Small Business Development Center. Centers are usually located on the campus of a university and serve existing and start-up businesses. Consulting and basic information from this organization is free.

Sales tax in every state varies. You must have a state tax number as a reseller. You collect sales tax for the state and then hand it over to them. Some states will let you pay a discounted amount for providing this service if you pay by a specific date. (Think of yourself as the revenue collector for the state.) Sales tax is not an expense to your business. I mention it here because you may have to place a cash or surety bond with the state. This is up-front cash needed to start your business that can be a large sum. If it is not planned for, you will short yourself somewhere else in the start-up phase. Contact your state's Department of Revenue office for an application and any information.

Supplies: You will need a multitude of items to wrap up a sale and make the sale happen. Bags, pricing tags, tissue, cleaning materials, labels, gift enclosure cards, gift boxes, shipping boxes, tape, ribbon, instruction booklets or flyers, and more. Every business will have some specific needs like the cold packs for the chocolate truffles at the gourmet chocolate store.

Bags that the customers use to take their purchase out of the store can be simple kraft paper bags with a label or private stamp. Many bookstores have eliminated using bags as much as possible for environmental reasons. Book and food stores sell cloth bags with their logos printed on them for customers to carry away their purchase and advertise the store.

The packaging of the purchase needs to run smoothly and support your store image. Walk through a sale in your mind and with friends far in advance of opening to plan your needs. Some materials take several weeks to print or assemble and can't be relegated to a last-minute decision. Wholesalers of materials fill such a gap if you need it. Check the Yellow Pages for paper suppliers, box manufacturers and such. Sometimes these supplies are represented at trade shows you attend for your industry.

S.C. on Credit Cards: This stands for Service Charge on Credit Cards. Obtaining a merchant number from a bank is fairly simple for retailers. It is the discount percentage that causes a problem for the retailer. The discount percentage is the amount you pay the bank for processing your credit card transactions. A customer pays you with a credit card. Actually, the credit card company pays you when your card transactions are deposited.

You can now have much of this process automated with automatic deposit. You have seen the machines everywhere you go. A swipe of the credit card through the card reader and your purchase is approved and documented. At the end of the day, you enter specific codes to balance out your sales and refunds, transfer the day's business to the credit card transfer company and, in 24 hours, the funds are deposited into your account.

You usually purchase the machines from your bank. Some cash register and electronic equipment companies handle them.

Shop for a bank to handle this. Small stores are usually charged a higher percentage than larger volume stores for handling their credit card transactions. Automating the process brings down this percentage because the bank's physical handling of paper is greatly reduced. This can offset the up-front cost of the card reader machines. Some banks offer lower percentages to the stores that are located near them. Banks located in or near large regional malls do this. I have seen a percentage as low as 1½ percent offered in this case. If you handle your purchases "the old way," you may pay well over 3 percent, (possibly 4 or 5 percent). I think this is robbery. You must shop for a bank to handle this. If you feel you must stay with the bank that does your loan, negotiate the best percentage you can get. Over time, as your sales volume increases, go back and ask for a lower rate. The percentage is based on volume of deposits.

When you do cash flow projections, multiply the percentage against sales. Not all of your sales will be paid for by credit card—the national average runs around 30 percent. If you are located in an area that has tourist and other out-of-town traffic, your percentage of sales made on credit cards will be higher, perhaps 45 or 50 percent, or more. Figure the percentage of projected sales and then multiply by your discount rate. That is your projected cost.

Bank Charges: Even if you have a loan with your bank, you will probably be charged on the activity of your checking account. With payroll checks, monthly payroll tax deposits, supplier payments, daily deposits and so on, a small store could easily spend $50 a month and more in charges. Banks charge for each item on the deposit as well as for each NSF check you write. Avoid paying for NSF (Non Sufficient Funds) charges. At $15, $17.50 or more for each check, it is wasted money. Plan your cash flow to avoid such problems. Talk to your vendors and get a couple of more days before sending the check in order to have the sales deposits to cover the checks. Every business has cyclical money needs. Arrange for a line of credit for high inventory purchase times.

Miscellaneous: Be careful what you lump into this category. Plan by putting $200 or so onto this line to cover yourself. When you are open, anything that consistently appears when you write out checks should have a category of its own to be tracked properly. When the monthly Profit and Loss Statement is compiled along with the Balance Sheet, you want the best possible picture of your operation. If you see $362 in the Miscellaneous category one month and don't know what it is, you have to go back through the General Ledger journal to know the reason for the $362.

Interest on Loan: You borrow future profits when you obtain a loan. The cost for doing this is the interest you pay the bank or other investor. This is an expense. The principle part of the payment is not an expense. It is your future profits you borrowed to get started. It takes profit to pay back a loan.

This is the most difficult and upsetting part of a business for many people. When they look at the bottom of the P & L statement and see a profit but know they don't have any cash, they are confused and upset. If you look at your balance sheet and see the loan amount going down, that is where the cash goes. Cash also goes to pay sales tax you collected for the state, as well as federal and state taxes you withheld from your employee's checks. Those items are not your money and that is why they do not appear on the P & L. They are liabilities that appear on your balance sheet.

Unfortunately, accountants do a poor job of explaining this to clients. I have held many a hand after clients met with their accountant and left frustrated about having asked questions without understanding the answers.

The next part of the Cash Flow Projection Form deals with those items that do not appear on the P & L. They do affect your cash flow, however. The loan principle payment has been discussed. To calculate interest and principle, use an accounting software program or an amortization chart. The bank can help you here.

Capital Purchases: These are those large equipment purchases that you will depreciate over time. This is cash going out all at once. However, you do not expense the purchase in the time period you make it. Depreciation occurs as a noncash expense against these items. Since most assets are purchased with borrowed money, the expense of the items occurs over time. Your accountant will set up depreciation schedules for the various items.

Assets such as fixtures, computers, furniture, cash registers, and lights are depreciable. Plan for them cash-wise when you want to make the purchase.

Other Start-Up: These are large purchases like your leasehold improvements to create your store image. Just like an asset, you depreciate this over a period of time. The leasehold improvement cost appears as an asset on your balance sheet.

Owner's Draw: If you are a sole proprietor, plan for a draw out of the business. Sole proprietorship is not the same thing as a corporation. Sole proprietors draw funds from the business and at the end of the year report the business activity on their personal tax return. A corporation files its own return. If you elect to be an S-Corp, then you as the owner are an employee of the corporation. In that case, your salary is projected along with other salaries.

A cash flow form shows how cash flows through the business. Add up all of the incoming cash:

> Cash on Hand
> +   Sales/Receipts
> +   Collections
> +   Loans/Other Injections
> _____
> Total Cash on Hand

Sales/Receipts and Collections added together make up Total Cash Receipts.

Cash on Hand is money you put into the business. Sales/Receipts are your projected sales for each month. Collections are monies from bad debts you have collected. Projecting this gives you a realistic look at cash flow. Figure about ½ percent of sales as bad debts (which is a little high for most retailers). Collect half of that figure the following month on the projection form.

Add up all the expenses on the Subtotal/Expenses line. Add up the next four items and add them to Subtotal/Expenses. That total is Total Cash Paid Out. Subtract that figure from Total Cash on Hand to arrive at Ending Cash. Filling out the cash flow form without any Cash on Hand or Loans will show you how much cash you need. (You can ignore interest for the moment.) The highest negative figure is how much money the business need. To do the best projections, calculate cash flow for one full year plus the start-up month. Take into account the seasonal needs of your business for inventory, staffing, supplies, insurance (increase your insurance when your inventory goes up,) bank charges, marketing and advertising expenses.

Cash Flow Projecting

At any time in your business, you can make a cash flow projection for the next few months, including considering discounts on invoices. Here is how:

1. Have all your outstanding payables available to calculate. Separate trade/purchases of inventory out from others (printing, advertising, etc.).

2. Chart out your monthly sales projections (from OTB plan).

3. Put the figures for A/Ps under the appropriate months (of when they are due).

4. Figure the gross profit and then figure the cash discounts on the A/Ps to see the difference.

5. Do the same with the future OTB dollar amounts. Remember to reduce the retail dollar amount of OTB to a cost figure. Use your maintained markon to make the calculation.

Having a quick overview like this can help you plan when you can and can't take discounts, although, as mentioned before, the advantages of taking them warrant using your line of credit.

ACTION LIST FOR CHAPTER 4

• Review suggested Chart of Accounts (in Appendix II) and develop your own based on your operation.

• Make an area in your office, file drawer, or a separate file holder for financial data such as your sales tracking, invoices matched to Purchase Orders received, Profit and Loss Statements from your accountant.

• Owners of new stores should interview and select an accountant after getting referrals from trusted professionals in your network.

• Copy or adapt the Deposit Reconciliation Form in Appendix III for use every day.

• Practice projecting cash flow for your store after planning your OTB. Purchases will be the result of OTB less your markon percentage, entered in the month following receipt of goods.

Chapter 5

Merchandising Techniques: In-Store Strategies

This chapter addresses working and reworking the merchandising techniques of how a particular group of merchandise in your store relates to all of the merchandise. The appearance and grouping of merchandise supports its ability to perform—by creating sales and turning at a high enough rate to make a profit. Here, we want to address how you put together the right assortment of merchandise, how you select price ranges, what the components of merchandise selection criteria are and how you present it to the customer.

The next chapter, Buying Strategies, analyzes the figures of the store to replace inventory and continue or improve merchandise performance.

Remember, you looked at the policies needed to support your store's philosophy and define your store's image. Various timing and environmental components to consider throughout your planning process were mentioned. You also looked at policies needed to support your store's philosophy and define your store's image.

Now, let's look at the other components of a store—planning tools for the best product mix and visual appearance.

PRODUCT MIX

Development of product mix comes out of the policies you have set for your store. Let's look closer at some of these to get a stronger feel for developing your own product mix. Some of these were mentioned earlier, briefly, for the OTB planning process. Your product mix supports and creates the store image, conveying your concept to the customer.

What is happening here? Working the dollar figures from your OTB into actual stock assortments is meaningful to your concept. Your concept creates the basis of your product mix. Do I need to remind you how dangerous it is to shop your market without detailed planning? And you thought that getting through the first chapter would end that discussion. Wrong! Going through the steps presented here increases your odds for success.

Let's take the policy categories one by one and look at them in another light. Then we can define actual product mixes from our detailed descriptions of the store's concept and philosophy.

Price

The more important price is to the customer, the more you need to need to analyze your retail prices. What price points does your competition carry or what price ranges have been the most successful for your store? Watch for successful price points by department and subclass.

If your gift items at $35 and above stay on the shelf for months and the items in the $18 to $25 range sell the most, then analyze potential purchases in the light of that fact. Even if you don't track most of your inventory by item, you and your staff can stay well aware of what items don't move when you clean and move them around in the store trying to find the magic spot. You mark an item down. Perhaps you were greedy and didn't take a deep markdown the first time and now the age of the item shows. You still own it.

When working on your OTB plan, notice which departments and/or subclasses are more price sensitive than others. Every buyer needs to do this, no matter what type of store. Give close consideration to those areas that display such sensitivity when placing orders.

Take your notes from market and list the items you are seriously considering from an objective merchandiser's viewpoint. List the retail price of each item (per piece as the selling price). Now list the quantities you were considering. When you add up the total number of items by retail price, have you selected well in your customer's comfortable price range? If not, go back and review that selection.

Let's go back to the figures cited earlier. Having a few items in the $30 to $35 range can be all right. Certain customers of yours like this type of goods. They are great for rounding out the assortment because of what they stand for—better quality or more trendy style. Think of these items as the icing on the cake and remember that too much icing and little cake makes for no substance and a sick customer. So, without the stock in the price range your customers say they are willing to pay for, you will lose those customers.

Always look at who your customer is through research. Don't wait until you are stuck with all that fluff on the shelves you thought was so cute in the showroom. This is a very good reason why you should not write orders in the showroom until you have good plans and are proficient and confident with them. The learning curve here is unpredictable from one person to the next. Some people develop the instincts necessary to respond with accuracy sooner than others. Even instincts, though, can't act as a substitute for information. Note that I said "respond with accuracy."

When looking at your customer in relation to your merchandise, price is a major consideration. Even if you have targeted a segment with a large disposable income, price is an issue. Spending money is related to value, not just the dollar amount on the price tag. If an item does not look worth the price, it won't matter whether or not people can afford it. They won't buy it.

Consumers are very educated about their shopping. Do not confuse price and affordability. The item must stand on its own.

Quality

Quality deserves further discussion. This is probably the most important aspect about making a purchase to consumers in the '90s. Companies in the past have produced poor quality and expected the consumer to view the product as disposable. They took advantage of our consuming-oriented society. American corporations have slowly woken up to face a new consumer, who is smart, gets information before making purchases and asks a lot of questions.

Watch how customers look at an item. They want to know what it does, how it does it, and how is it made. I have watched customers look at the inside of garments, underneath furniture and pick up large mechanical items to learn more about the product. I have also watched customers returning an item because close inspection of the product at home disappointed them.

You must set your standards of quality. Discuss quality with your staff, telling them what you look for in products. Their understanding of this will help sell items and enable them to give you feedback when something doesn't meet that standard based on customer reaction.

If your store is a volume price store with no frills, OK, but know what ranges of quality your vendors provide. Whether you are a new store or existing, shop other stores and look closely at the vendors. Shopping in other cities can also be useful.

If an item goes above or below the quality policy you have set, before purchasing any amount ask yourself whether it really fits in with the total assortment. If you are looking to begin changing the image of the store, small tests would be wise to feel out the customer for their dollar "votes."

Breadth and Depth of Assortment

The number of and depth of styles carried is an important part of your product mix. Usually higher priced goods are more appealing when they appear unique and in limited quantity. Review the broad and narrow assortment definition in the first chapter on OTB planning to help you with this.

Imagine walking into a store with a large selection of crystal items. Many styles, shapes and types of items in crystal are on display throughout the store. Only one or two of any one item exists in the product mix. This is a broad and shallow assortment. The customer willing to pay a higher price for a unique and special item feels that the item twinkling in their eye truly is special. This is the basis of a company like Sharper Image. They present a wide selection of electronic toys, gadgets, life-style equipment. They don't present five different excercycles, just one they believe is the best to suit their customer.

Rows of the same item at a high price (remember, everything is relative) lessen the special feeling of such an item. Yes, there are times to pile it high such as a sale with massive markdowns or a discount operation. Think! Is the price lower in those situations? It probably is, isn't it?

Think through the selection. When you select a product group, decide in what department you will track it. You may give it its own subclass department to see quickly how your customer responds to it. When you are making your purchase decision, select the best styles to present it. Add up the cost and retail price totals. What percentage of the whole department does it represent?

If you are selecting items based on your feelings of a new trend, make this a small percentage of the department, no more than 10 percent of the BOM when it will come into the store. If your customer jumps on new trends, then you are safer with a larger percentage. The merchandise will then make a bigger statement in the store.

Visualize the number of units in the store. Walk through your store and pick out where the merchandise will go. Before finalizing the dollar amount of your purchase(s), be sure the number of units accomplishes a goal. Are you adding to a strong selling trend? Presenting new items? Pushing a promotion? Visualizing may be easier for you by looking at your racks and shelves. The more experience you have buying and selling, the easier this becomes. New store owners need to shop the competition and stores in other cities to know what merchandise on the selling floor will look like. Ask yourself if it will fill the purpose you have set up.

Re-add the figures after any selection changes. Yes, this takes time, but it is your inventory and store image we're talking about. Massage it until it is right. Feel blocked? Walk away from it for a while; work on the floor with your staff where the most valuable information exists—your customers. Always remember that the decisions about broad and shallow or narrow and deep assortments will come to you. Since retailing doesn't stand still, there's always something for you to watch that will give you a key or a clue to a decision.

Brand Offerings

Brands are those labels highly recognized by customers nationally. Brands also are names companies develop as a private label. The products are manufactured for them under specific quality and price guidelines. Esprit, Wilson, Levi, Chanel, Starbuck's (coffee) and Fieldcrest are all examples of brands. Again, look to your target market research before deciding whether or not to carry brand names.

Evaluate how important brand names will be to your customer. Also, who else around you carries certain brands? Another option is finding a brand people like but is not carried in your area. If you don't want to be a "me too" store, then look for vendors that will give you the styling and item selection you are looking for to support your store concept.

There is that term again—store concept. You will decide incorrectly occasionally. You know that your concept is on target as you receive the customer's dollar votes. Listen to what those customers ask for. If they aren't vocal, ask them yourself from time to time.

Brands can present specific problems and opportunities for the independent retailer. Minimums to place orders and reorders are increasingly raised, causing a vendor to be more of your OTB dollars than you may be comfortable with. Why? You may have to buy styles you don't think fit into your product mix, which will become markdowns, dragging down your stockturn and reducing your ability to reorder the best sellers or new goods.

Unfortunately and fortunately, an independent is more flexible than a large store, but having to drop vendors because the minimum makes them unprofitable always hurts a store owner. However, too many times, I have seen owners that stick with a vendor for the other styles, ignoring the fact that the vendor has become unprofitable for them. Analyze your vendor figures to base your buying decision. Using vendor analysis is discussed in the next chapter.

Carrying a brand name will affect your marketing (it should if you really think about it), which in turn affects your inventory. Well-known brands will be an advantage when you know that your potential customer responds positively because you carry them. They take a prominent position in your marketing pieces and can be the basis of successful promotions.

Another point to consider in relation to the placement of orders against your OTB concerns the importance of any one vendor. Having most of your dollars tied up with a brand name vendor leaves you high and dry when you aren't shipped. This occurs for many reasons and more frequently than any retailer likes to think about! This certainly makes sense to you, since you have learned that too little stock means lost sales.

Add up your orders with a vendor. Look at it in relation to the percentage of each department it affects and the whole store. Imagine what your store would look like if 20 percent of your inventory replacement didn't arrive in your store on time or at all! You should be cringing!

Exclusivity

Whether you have decided that exclusivity is important to your store or not, you will still need to evaluate the amount of purchases that go into those exclusive items. You need to ask yourself how much depth is enough to make a statement. You need to maintain a good balance so you don't get hurt if the vendor fails you. So, how to evaluate it?

Consider the amount of space you have, your fixtures, and what the exclusive merchandise's purpose is to the store. Let's take a closer look.

Store space: A small space of 600 square feet can house a lot of goods, depending on the items. It won't take much to make a statement with inventory in a well-laid-out store. If the exclusive item is something basic, don't put it out all at once, but just in enough depth to get the customer's attention and to sell. You will have to replenish the stock frequently if it is a basic offered in various forms or colors and priced such that it is an easy sell. Some items need only a display, allowing you to sell the stock from a drawer or stockroom. Accessory items like fine leather goods, specialized electronics, luggage accessories and items for monogramming are examples.

If newness is the purpose of the item, then prominence becomes important and the quantity depends on the price, store concept and such. Some trend-setting items catch on quickly. If you tie your exclusivity into a time frame (receiving shipments before other stores), stock in the quantity you believe makes the statement. Place enough stock to sell while you wait for a reorder.

This might be a dozen or ten dozen, depending on your customer, location's traffic, price and other items available. This is not meant to be vague. You can not select any items for the store without considering the whole store.

Again, how much have you invested in the exclusive items in relation to the total department and store? A couple of percent is a lot. If your inventory for the month is $36,000 then $720 could be a lot of goods, depending on the retail per piece and what else is in the store. If the item is a $10 retail, that's six dozen of the item. A mall with strong foot traffic will eat up that amount of a hot item in no time. Point: Think it through in terms of your customer's buying habits and store's traffic.

Example: A small decorative and gift store client was selling lace collars before they were hot. She kept selling them as they became popular. She was missing out on the opportunity to make a good profit on the item. She only bought small quantities and let them sell down before she placed a reorder.

The goal: Take advantage of her foresight on the saleability of the item and the great price her collars were over the competition. (She had found a good source and on top of it was getting a whopping 65 percent markon!)

How to make it work: We calculated her sell-through on the collars by figuring how long it took her to sell past orders. I felt confident customers would respond to an increased selection. Then she would really have fun with it by running a special promotion with direct mail and ad support. A storewide sale was coming up and I convinced the owner to feature the collars as an item. She place a six dozen order—six times what she had ever placed before!

Goal achieved: The goods hit replenishing the floor stock and expanding it with additional styles increasing the selection. Normal sales picked up on their own from customers responding to the larger selection. The owner placed signage in the window noting "wide selection of lace collars," placed an ad for the sale with the collars featured as a special purchase, and sent cards to her mailing list customers. She sold four dozen in two weeks—quite an improvement over selling a dozen a month. The special offer was minimal since we knew she had a hot item not quite at its peak of popularity.

Result: Profit.

Relationship to Fashion Trends

The previous example describes more than a store's use of a form of exclusivity and evaluation of the purchase amount of an item into the product mix. This store had customers that weren't the trendiest in town but appreciated finding unique items before other people did at a reasonable price. The owner used much of her time at market looking for items that would fill that need and spent up to 25 percent of the OTB in those items.

The store's layout accommodated merchandising items in with her basic decorative goods. This amount of her inventory was always changing, giving her clientele reason to come back continually to see what was new. This is a goal for any store, whether you offer the trendiest of goods in town or mainly basic items. Even a camping store has goods that change. The basic items have innovations continually. Our world is ever changing and so will be the character of your store. It must to survive.

Basic Stock Maintenance

Many stores have basic stock items: food, clothing, hardware, auto parts, pet supplies, sports, optical, plants. Face it. People have similarities, which create the need for basic items. You will find items in your store that can be classified as basics. A bath store sold basics like shower liners, soap dishes, little plastic nubby things that keep your soap from drying out (which had a markup of about 70 percent!), pretty guest soaps, and some pieces of hardware. It is important to maintain enough inventory to satisfy sales. Basics must be in stock or you lose sales.

Let's look at an example to understand carving out enough OTB to keep your basic stock in a healthy position during its peak selling time. Let's say that a specialty store previously sold 12 percent of the total sweater sales in a basic item the year before, say a turtleneck. This year basics look really good with a couple of new fabrics and great colors. You figure the increase of the department and subclass affecting this item, and you decide to make this basic 14 percent of your sales instead of 12 percent. Multiply out the dollars to know how much OTB will be devoted to the basic turtleneck.

Example: Last year sales on turtleneck = $11,200 over a three month period.

You plan an 8% increase in sweaters making the dollar amount for this sub-class $12,096.

Now, you want to have at least three dozen each month in a new fashion fabric in your turtleneck assortment.

This allows you to carry at least two colors each month You decide on one basic and one fashion color.

The cost per piece is $10.50, and the selling price $22. To cover the three month period (108 pieces at $22), $2,376 of your OTB goes to this one item alone. Another way to look at it is 19.64 percent of this subclass. Depending on the size of the store and traffic, this may be acceptable. Thirty-six pieces hitting the store each month probably won't make much of an impact. Since it is a new fabric, you may want to test it at this level for the first month and plan higher levels for the following months. Talking to your staff can help in this decision with their reaction to the style and colors.

Calculate your average selling price for this category (sweaters for this example) from the previous year's sales. A start-up can calculate the average selling price of the product selected. Divide the average selling price into the planned OTB figure. The result is the number of units you will buy. Visualize those units on your racks, shelves and display props. Now think about the three dozen of the new turtleneck. Does it still seem like enough? This is a process of stepping out of a narrow focused decision to be a better buyer.

Playing back and forth with the dollars and units helps to buy items and groups of items in relation to the product mix desired. This shows you how to work within the OTB plan to develop a strong product mix appropriate for your store. Flexibility and specific structure do work hand-in-hand in an OTB plan. Use these as watchwords for your own plans.

Many times I have referred to visualizing stock situations. "Seeing" your store in your mind helps to create a total store with a complete picture of balanced inventory. If visualization doesn't come easy to you, shop other stores. Count the number of pieces on shelves and mark off the length of shelves by "walking it off." Shop other stores to count goods and actually see similar merchandise presented on racks, shelves, tables, walls, bins or whatever. Ask yourself, as a customer, if the statement is made—new arrival, new trend, promotional goods, big markdown for clearance—what? Practice this in other stores and your own. Watch customers in your own store for reactions and again, do the same in competitors stores and in stores when you travel. Retailing is a continual process, as you create your plan, business continues and adjustments will become a part of the process. This is "professional retail punting!" And it is truly an art.

This leads us into discussing the visual presentation of goods in further detail. Visual merchandising encompasses much more than "display" as you will see.

VISUAL MERCHANDISING

Goal: Arrangement of merchandise to sell. You want to incite the motivation to buy and convey your store's message of who you are. Then customers know what to expect and why they'll return to shop again. Visual merchandising includes store planning, physical layout and the display of your merchandise. Store planning is addressed first since this relates to your floor layout and the design of your store.

Layout of Store

Here, we are looking at the location and amount of space allotted to each merchandise department, as well as the nonselling areas. The layout must support your merchandising plan. Larger departments (in sales) usually need larger amounts of space. A decreasing department would lose some of its space.

   Points to consider:
   • Image of store
   • Customer preferences (you will know from customer profile)
   • Competitors' layouts
   • Stock capacity of store itself
   • Merchandise changes in departments

Sales per square foot of selling space is an evaluation tool. Calculate this figure by dividing the total sales by the number of square feet. Do this for the total store and each department. This is a measure of productivity. Look for increases year-to-year as well as decreases. This helps you decide how much space departments and subclasses need in order to perform. This is another guideline, besides total sales dollars, of your customer's wants and needs.

Take the sales per square foot into consideration when remodeling by evaluating the needs of each department in relation to sales produced. Also look at this as a way to push more sales out of a department. Perhaps the goods have suffered in sales due to poor location and exposure to the customer. The necessity of increasing turn to get more sales per square foot will prove imperative in the '90s when you see specialty chains pushing over $400 per square foot annually.

Design and Decor

Your selection of design materials communicates to the customer your store concept. The customer looks in the window and into the store. They will comprehend the type of store you are—high end, fun experience, volume price, niche product/market selection, and so on. Using design components appropriate to a different store type and customer confuses your potential customer.

Color and lighting are very important in the shopping experience. Look at the following list and think about these elements in relation to color and quality and what they can say to the customer.

- Style of fixtures
- Overall design style: traditional vs. contemporary, eclectic, tropical, etc.
- Carpet
- Wall coverings
- Dividers
- Wall hangings
- Planters
- All fixtures -

    Shelves

    Display racks

    Counters

    Mannequins

    Other display units

- Lighting

If you remodel your facility, remember to support the change throughout your total marketing plan—direct marketing pieces, advertising, promotions and in-store presentation. Change your color theme. Change it on your business cards and direct mail pieces. Change from contemporary to traditional type fonts if appropriate. Change your paper colors, internal signs, stationery, mailers, everything.

Changes in image can increase sales overall. Upgrading can also increase the Average Unit Sales. Stores become old looking, fixtures and decor wear out. Customers respond by losing interest and going to new stores. Remodeling then becomes a marketing tool to regenerate interest and increase sales.

Working with an outside design specialist can be a great move, but remember to temper it with your own good business sense. Creativity for creativity's sake doesn't help your store's presentation or growth. Many designers produce great-looking designs, but they aren't functional enough for retail. Can the customer get to the merchandise? Is the merchandise displayed to feature it? Is there a traffic flow that leads the customer through the store? Are the windows properly lighted? Will the sales desk be positioned to help you prevent shoplifting? Are the dressing rooms large enough for your type of merchandise? Are they well-lit? (Don't make them blaring but have them bright enough to see well and make the merchandise look good.) If you need bins, can customers get to the bottom bin easily or is it too low? If you have many older customers, this could be a problem.

Look to fixtures that are easy to care for, cost-effective and flexible in usage for additional changes. Keep in mind the customer who will still want convenience and ease of shopping. Custom fixtures may be an answer for you. Look at your concept and the investment. Calculate your sales projections to know that this is viable. A food store wanted to present a new way to buy gourmet and health items a decade ago. They offered ingredients in bins allowing customers to buy as much or as little as they wanted. Their bulk bins were custom-made for them based on their research of ease of scooping out the ingredients. Since this was the core of their concept, their up-front expense was necessary. Ready-made containers at lower costs were found for some of the ingredients. This offset the custom fixture costs.

Security is key for every store. Many people, especially those new to retail, ignore this. Unfortunately for you, even experts ignore it when developing store design and layout. A past client had a "retail designer" draw up plans for the store. One quick look at the blueprints was all that it took me to see:

1. The dressing rooms were poorly placed to ensure security measures by the sales staff.

2. The lighting placement failed to highlight the merchandise, display areas and the dressing rooms. (Customers hate dressing in the dark!)

Deadline stress overpowered my client and she didn't press for changes.

Two thefts occurred in the first month of business due to inability to watch the floor. The dressing rooms, which had not been moved, didn't promote customer service and prevented any kind of security.

From this example, you can see that you really need to do your homework to work with designers. If you are not an experienced retailer, find one that is willing to look at your plans and offer their opinion. Choose carefully, evaluating that person for the value they can offer you from their experience.

Another client hired an architect who went solo from a residential firm they had worked with before. Again, lighting became an issue, as well as not knowing where to put the sales desk. Fortunately the client did her homework. Between the two of us, we did the store fixturing layout and lighting. The architect didn't know how to position the slat wall. He wanted to make the front window way too small, as well as eliminate a side window! We fixed these problems quickly in the blueprint stage. The worst problem after that occurred when expensive, Italian, handmade accent lights were delivered. We only needed inexpensive lights to go behind cutout masks that were part of the store decor. The client made the architect take the light fixtures back. Good for her.

The best watchword here is to do your homework—shop competitors, shop other cities, put yourself in the position of the customer to evaluate the space. Always keep your concept and customer profile in mind, asking yourself if a certain design or fixture makes sense in those terms.

Store Display

Most people picture store display in the library of mental images if you say "visual merchandising." As we are discussing here, it is much more than that. The integral nature of design and decor with store display is seen in the fixtures and lighting needed to support your store display.

There are two vehicles for store display:

- Windows
- Interior

Telling a story paves the road to success. You can highlight, instruct and more in both spaces. The windows get a potential customer through the door. The interior display creates the impulse buy, point of purchase interest, supports a promotion theme and enhances decor.

Windows attract, calling to the customer, enticing them in. Once inside, the story continues, more stories are told and your salespeople carry out the parts of the story, bringing important pieces together and to a close. A sale is made.

Let's look at each in more detail.

Windows

Get the potential customer to stop and want to come inside. Not all retail utilizes this, which you will see on a stroll through a local mall. Some mall locations are totally open sales floors from the front to the back of the store.

Keys to putting together windows:
- Display newness (trends) in items, colors or concepts.
- Sell a promotion.
- Demonstrate a method or some other "how-to."
- Tell the customer price if it fits your store concept.

Sparse windows generally indicate higher priced specialty items inside the store. Note expensive merchandise in stores on Rodeo Drive, Michigan Avenue and similar streets.

Cluttered, packed windows equate lower price, budget merchandising and little or no sales service. Well-merchandised windows—art, exhibiting handmade pieces, pottery, scarves, jewelry—let the merchandise make a statement. No theme and a multitude of product is to be avoided except by bargain basement operations.

Do not look at either of these points as good or bad. Ask yourself what is right for your store. If your customer is looking for fun or a traditional shopping environment, then you will know which way to go.

Guidelines for Productive Windows

Windows need to be productive. They work for you as part of your real estate.

- Use timely merchandise; what is in current demand or newest.
- Choose the quantity of items based on the store image.
- Know that you have adequate stock available.

Don't make your customer angry. If it is in the window, it needs to be available for purchase. When an item sells down, change the windows or take that item out. On this last point, the type of retail operation defines what is adequate for your stock. Depending on the store concept, image and item, this may be four pieces or four dozen.

The stores that don't have windows still need to entice shoppers to come in. You need to use fixturing that highlights. Group a few pieces of an item with accessory items. Another way to get a customer's attention is grouping a lot of one or similar items together, merchandised as stock. When customers look in, they see the beginning of the store with a strong statement of what else will be found inside. Pier One stores have done this very successfully, even in stores that have windows. Note that most of their windows are very large and the stores have high ceilings allowing for big furniture displays.

Interior Display

Use your interior display to support all your other efforts in marketing and themes presented in the windows. Themes in your direct mail, special promotions, print advertisements or radio are repeated and emphasized encouraging and promoting the image of the store and the goods themselves.

In this field of merchandising as well as others, there are experts that will assist you and train you to see the opportunities and intricacies of successful display. Some professionals freelance outside of their department store job or full-time.

Placement plays a large part in success for the small, independent store. Item sales will benefit greatly when placed in a point of purchase position in the store. This area may be at or very near where the sale is written or next to the selling floor space. The customer will not have to go far to find an item that interests them.

The display boosts impulse purchases and aids sales staff in a soft-selling approach. Salespeople can supply more information about an item that a customer spots next to the cash register when they make a purchase.

Items can certainly appear in many other areas of the store. Use your common sense as to what story you are telling and benefit you want to achieve.

Remember the change frequency of the displays. Consider your type of merchandise and purpose at the time. Letting displays get old in your store is a crime. If you sell out or become low in stock due to a promotion before your regular display change day, change it immediately! You will only frustrate your customers when they discover you have displayed an item no longer available. Remind your staff to watch this very closely.

Types of Displays and Their Purposes

• Assortments: Showing the customer one of each available style in a section of stock. Basics work best here and can serve as a way to inform the customer of the selection and price of the items. Basic turtleneck pullovers in different style variations or cartoon mugs are examples.

• Item Displays: Featuring a particular item, either one piece or a selection, works to highlight the item and inform the customer of other options. A platter in different sizes or selection of colors in a candle exemplify item displays.

• Racks: These allow customers to select items themselves. Use T-stands or other smaller racks, or shelf units that allow you to feature new items, promotional items or selections. Signage indicating the point of the display—color, sale price, new trend—should accompany this interior display for success.

• Vignettes: Show how a customer might use the items or put them together with other related items when purchased. This format provides great potential for storytelling and add-on selling opportunities for your sales staff.

There are many techniques that are beyond the scope of this book. Experiment and shop other stores when you travel to learn new techniques from professional visual merchandisers. Think about what you like and don't like in your store. Just because it was in the window of a high-styled store on Madison Avenue doesn't make it right for your store image. Evaluate the display on its selling in terms of getting the story across. If you stopped in your tracks to look at it, ask yourself "why?"

Through visual merchandising, you communicate to your customer who and what you are. As your store evolves along with your customer you will look to using the described techniques to convey the changes in your store image.

CHANGING YOUR STORE'S IMAGE

Nothing stays the same. As your store grows, you will update your look, perhaps even change your focus. Customers move away and new consumers move into your trade area. As an area evolves so will you. Even if the trade area stays fairly stable, trends and tastes, needs and wants are not static. Your selling information will tell you what they vote in favor of and against.

These guidelines will help you through this process:

• Make the change gradually.

• Allow it to evolve.

- Change the assortment in relation to trends developing.
- Change quality standards.
- Change your pricing range.
- Use different display techniques and themes than those previously used.

Changing a store's image won't happen overnight and will be more difficult than building the image from the start. You will have to work with your product mix carefully to switch the look of the store from your initial presentation to the next. Use your OTB plans to the fullest to accomplish this.

When your store begins to show signs of age and trends around you have changed, it is time for a dramatic face lift. The merchandise, if handled properly, should have evolved. But your leasehold improvements over the last six or eight years have not. I am sure you have seen malls go through major overhauls after as little as ten years. Trends change faster than ever before now. Your store needs to change along with them.

CUSTOMER SERVICE AND SELLING TECHNIQUES

I have mentioned earlier that through flexibility, aggressiveness and good planning an independent retailer can out-merchandise the bigger stores. Customer service remains the most wieldy tool an independent can use against the bigger competition.

Customer Service

Subscribing to a formula of customer service and personal selling techniques will further your business more effectively and profitably than almost any of the advertising you will do. Store owners who have spent untold dollars on print (what most people think of as advertising) ads in newspapers and magazines will certainly vouch for this point.

We would need a separate dissertation on both these subjects to cover them fully. The following outlines and pointers will set you in motion.

What makes customer service?

1. Knowledgeable staff
2. Attitude of staff
3. Honesty
4. Etiquette
5. Communicating policies well

Selling Techniques

You can expand on any and/or all of these items to develop your own guidelines for hiring a staff. Once you have hired them you may want to train them to use the following attributes to develop good selling techniques.

- Product knowledge
- Interest in the customer
- Friendly attitude
- Honesty
- Generate feedback
- Be understanding, patient
- Keep it simple
- Create trust
- Good listener
- Enthusiastic
- Knowing the store, policies and philosophy
- Good at determining the wants of the customer

Use the following guidelines to create strong selling abilities in your staff. The first point, which anyone can learn, is the easiest way to sell. Considering these, you will recognize the need to share inventory information with your staff and encourage them to share customer response and ideas with you.

- Sell FAB—Features, Advantages, Benefits
- Anticipate objections
- Change customer belief, attitude or course of action
- Remember, all customers are different
- Trial closing
- Generate goodwill

ACTION LIST FOR CHAPTER 5

- Plan your product mix and price lines for your departments and subclasses.

- Write out your quality standards. You can use these guidelines in ads and for training staff on product.

- Target items that will be/are basics in your store. Plan out the number of pieces per month, plus the sales and inventory levels. Tally the amount of dollars this represents in your OTB monthly.

• Study competitors in your city and other cities for layout and display ideas—in-store and windows.

• Ask friends and/or professionals to critique your windows and POP (point of purchase, or your sales desk) area and tell you which displays they believe are attractive, eye-catching and encourage customer purchase.

• Set up regular meetings to review new incoming products with your staff.

Chapter 6

Buying Strategies: Putting Your System To Work

Your store is open. Sales are sending merchandise out. New purchases bring in new goods. A flow of merchandise is occurring every day. In this chapter, you learn how to use the information you have collected in your inventory system. You want to learn to guide your buyer's eye to see problems before they happen, make your good plans better and to find your future growth.

USING THE SALES AND PURCHASE PERFORMANCE REPORT

We will continue to work with the SPPR as we want your inventory to do just that—perform! As you move in and out of the reports and data, using the formulas you have already learned plus some new ones, your store performance will become practiced, polished and primed for protecting your investment and creating growth.

Growth in retail just doesn't happen, especially in the '90s. Competition is fierce, to use a trite saying, and the lions of the industry appear to be forever growing. It is tough for them, too, though on different levels. The independent retailer must continue to develop new strategies and use as many tricks of the trade as the lions.

Using the SPPR to Better Your Buying and Inventory Levels

What better source of tools than your Sales and Purchase Performance Report? There are more reasons than those already cited for keeping all these records.

What are you looking for on the SPPR, anyway?

- Inventory level—is it too high? Too low?
- Are sales making plan?
- What's the S/S Ratio in each department?
- What trend Is appearing in any of the merchandising components?—S/S Ratio? Avg. stock? Turn? Initial markon?
- What goods hit (were received) this month?
- What increases have occurred over last year?
- What decreases occurred?

101

- What percent of the whole is each department's sales?
- Are there changes in sales? What percent up or down from last year?
- Is the total store up or down over last year? And by what percent?

You have plotted out where you wanted to go. Are you getting there? And in the amount of time you projected?

The Importance of Stock Turnover

On the lower right-hand side of the SPPR, enter the turn for the period you are evaluating. In Chapter 3, Inventory Management, you learned how to track information and calculate the components of the SPPR. Now let's look at these analysis tools.

Stockturn is an enigma to many people. They take it for just the resulting figure after using the formula and then go no further, looking to the sky as though some great retail sun god would suddenly make it better.

Wrong! This is not a religious dissertation, but your guide to keep your fate in your own reliable hands. Information is the key. Here are a few more facts to look at how important it is to your store to manipulate your inventory to improve your stockturn.

Calculating the Stockturn

Remember, to figure the stock turnover rate you need:

- The beginning inventory for the period
- Each BOM for the months you are figuring
- The EOM for the period
- Total sales for the period

Example:

BOM for a three month period	$ 5,699.56
BOM for next month	$ 7,327.81
BOM for third month	$ 8,819.50
EOM of third month	$10,224.35
Total Sales	**$ 3,450.01**

The Average Stock for this example is:

$$\frac{\$32,071.22}{4} = \$8,017.81$$

Stockturn = Net Sales ÷ Average Stock

So:

Average Stock = (All BOM + EOM) ÷ number of months

Average Stock = $8,017.81

Turn = $3,450.01 ÷ $8,017.81

Turn = .43

Turn can be looked at for a period of time. The above example is one quarter. That means the inventory only turned .43 times for the quarter. We already know from using annual turn for our projections the performance level desired. Since this is only the turn for a period of a quarter, then what is the annual projected turn?

Multiply the result by four. In this example our projected annual turn is:

1.72

When calculating the three-month performance for your SPPR, you can now look at your original plans to see if you are on target. Is 1.72 turn enough for this department to make a profit?

What if you calculate the turn for one month or six months? How do you arrive at the projected annual turn? The following chart gives you a multiplication factor to use after you calculate stockturn.

Number of Months	Multiplying Factor
1	12
3	4
6	2

Use the multiplying factor to calculate the rate you are turning your merchandise. You can calculate your turn for each department, subclass and the whole store. Keeping up with industry reports helps your decision-making process through comparison to similar stores. Is your turn too slow or too fast? What do you do to increase your performance?

Stock That Turns Too Fast

A stock turnover rate that is too slow obviously means that you will not be profitable or profitable enough to make it worth the effort. **When stock turns too fast, some particular problems arise:**

1. You lose sales due to lack of inventory when the customer comes in to purchase.
2. You have freight costs that are too high.
3. You have higher handling costs in the store.

Most might think a fast stockturn is a great merchandising feat, yet these problems reduce your profitability. Balance is key. Here are tips to keep your turn on target for your store and types of merchandise:

Review your sales weekly. Watch the S/S Ratio closely. Doing this by department and subclass allows you to detect quickly your customer's interest. The projected turn clues you in to taking action. In the case of a stockturn that is too high, you risk losing sales due to inadequate selection or availability of products, making customers unhappy. They will go elsewhere. If the problem persists, they will tire of your store being out of stock and won't waste their time to check if you have what they want.

Fix this problem by finding which product areas are turning faster than others (a very good reason to use subclasses). Find similar additional products. Increase your order size if you are ordering so frequently you're almost out of stock when the order comes in. You may need to find other vendors with the products that are selling faster.

When the whole store is turning extremely fast, take care of the best areas first. Don't risk losing customers because your shelves are empty.

Always use your merchandising information to develop that delicate combination in each department and total store to have a fast enough turn to make you the most profitable.

Stock That Turns Too Slowly

We want to keep your stock performance at or near peak. How you buy inventory, mark it down, reorder, markon, are all part of your buying strategy. Slow stockturn hurts you faster than you can imagine. Correcting the damage takes you longer than the opposite. Let's concentrate on several inventory situations and look at the strategies to combat them.

1. Lower interest cost because your money needs have been lowered.

2. Reduce taxes on inventory (if your state has such a tax).

3. Reduce storage costs.

4. Reduce insurance costs.

5. Increase sales with fresh, more appealing merchandise always on the sales floor.

6. Help reduce markdowns because merchandise has less chance of becoming old.

You already understand these concepts and tactics in your planning process. Let's approach the problems of controlling your inventory through increasing your turn with the goal of peak performance in mind.

First, assume that your turn is not as high as your competition or the industry averages. What does this mean to your business? Remember that inventory supports sales. Absolutely! However, a good product mix in the right quantity at the right time is always the goal to create those sales. This is the foundation of strong stockturn. If your stockturn lags, analyze each department first.

- Does any one department stand out with an extremely low turn?
- Spot problems by looking for high S/S Ratios.
- Has there been a high influx of merchandise? Check your Purchase Journals and tally received goods.

List all your departments with the pertinent information in columns across a sheet of paper, (or look at the recap in the computer program). Add each component to figure the average of each for the total store—stockturn, S/S Ratio, store inventory and markon. This quick look will tell you the story of whether one or two departments (and subclasses in those departments) are the problem area or whether it is the total store. This can be a chart in a spreadsheet program or use your SPPRs.

Actions to Improve Stockturn

Whether you are looking at storewide or departmental stockturn, you can act in the following ways:

1. Reduce the inventory with a markdown—this reduces the value of the inventory and boosts sales because the items are at a more desirable selling price. Businesses with two or more stores can target items not selling in one store and transfer them to the store where those items are selling better.

2. Buy in smaller quantities—this replenishes inventory more often and keeps you "closer to the vest."

3. Promote to increase sales—this can help reduce the amount of inventory in stock.

4. Reevaluate current OTB plans to prevent further imbalance of goods and product mix.

Within each of these strategies, many other valuable strategies and techniques exist. Each contains many tools that will assist you in controlling your inventory and protecting, even boosting, your profits. As a store owner and buyer, remember that nothing is static once your store is open. Retail moves constantly. You need to set your thinking to anticipate trends and react quickly to the data produced in your store. Inventory management and these strategies are your tools that allow you to react fast and with precision.

MARKDOWNS

This is Not a Dirty Word in Retailing Language

Problems arise when you have improperly purchased inventory in stock that must be moved out in order to have fresh new goods for your customers. You might simply be overbought, a condition every small store owner must work to avoid. Even the best buyers have items that are "dogs." They stare back at you with the cruelest of grins from your shelves and racks, daring you to take the deepest markdown you can to move them out.

Indiscriminately marking down goods doesn't help. Which department is turning the slowest compared to what it should be doing? If you are tracking subclass information, then take a hard look there for what sections of the department are slow. Usually any "dogs" will let you know they're there quickly as you pass them daily in the store. Utilize a staff meeting to scrutinize merchandise for markdowns. Your sales staff can provide you with valuable information. Computer programs should prompt you on items with slow sell-through.

Sell-through is the amount of time it takes to sell out of an item. No item truly sells out (rarely). Consumer behavior is such that the last piece stays on the shelf as though something were wrong with it. If you track items on the perpetual inventory form or on computer, it's easy to spot those "dogs" and see their sell-through. Take a markdown accordingly.

A word to the wise: Take the deepest markdown appropriate on slow-moving goods the first go around. Don't test the waters to see what will happen.

When a tree falls in the forest, do you know if it makes a sound even though no one is there to hear it? Chances are, you also can't guess what you could have made if you hadn't taken a big markdown on an item. The point here is this; move the goods out to make room for fresh. Don't waste your time and energy thinking that you could have made a couple of dollars more with a shorter markdown. You can't guess what the sales rate would have been at a lower price.

Example:

Item #223 in Department 12, Subclass 109

Original price— $ 79.90

First markdown price—$49.00

12 were in stock for five weeks without a sale.

You mark them down for a weekend sale, put signs in the windows, an easel at the entrance of the store and properly sign the shelves. Nine sell over the weekend! Great!

Hopefully the rest will be gone over the next week. The moral of the story is that you shouldn't think that you would have had more that the $441 in sales (9 x $49) if you had only marked them to $59 (just over a 25 percent reduction in price.) You might have only sold five pieces giving you only $295 (5 x $59) in sales. The other seven might dribble out over the next month.

Think of what shabby markdown goods do to the appearance of your store. Packages show wear from being picked up and handled. Poorly packaged items may break, chip or become scratched. All sorts of products become soiled from customer handling. And the longer they stay on the shelves, the shabbier they will truly become, begging further markdown. Your regular customers will see this and may decide to reduce the frequency of their visits to your store.

Taking the markdown to move it out of inventory provides dollars needed to purchase strong-selling items and/or fresh, new items.

When you borrow money to buy inventory, you pay interest on that money. As unsold inventory sits, those dollars tick away in interest. Tying up those borrowed dollars by refusing to mark down the inventory won't increase your turn. Worse, it costs you more money overall to keep your store open.

Guidelines for Taking Markdowns

- Stimulate sales of slow-moving or inactive stock
- Dispose of broken assortments or sets
- Provide additional OTB for new goods
- Meet a competitor's price
- Increase customer traffic

Use these to aid your selection of stock markdowns, as well as why and when you need to take the markdown.

DO EVERYTHING IN YOUR POWER TO PREVENT BEING OVERBOUGHT

A word about being overbought. Continually working with your merchandising information and the SPPR should keep you more than well informed of the movement of your inventory. Good buyers never place orders up to their OTB figure for any one period. Doing so prevents you from taking advantage of "hot" or new items that can benefit the store's product mix and profits. Such items are opportunities, and it is your responsibility to the ever-present bottom line to make the opportunity possible.

Watching weekly sales and comparing them to your projected sales helps you monitor the quantity of incoming goods. Look at your open purchases to cancel or delay shipments if you don't believe you will make your sales projections. If what was once a strong trend is on the downswing, work with your vendors to get out of merchandise not shipped. Any orders not in your store a few days from the cancel date should be canceled.

When you are overbought and those goods hit the store without the sales to move them, markdowns are the result even if the merchandise is fairly good. Having too much inventory, slows your turn, creating more markdowns, which eats away at your gross margin. The end result is reduced profit, no profit or a loss for the operation. In your head, remember—you are a seller, not a "buyer."

BUYING IN SMALLER QUANTITIES

The second way to increase stockturn has to do with buying "closer to the vest." To do so aids your keeping inventory in line and reducing the need for more drastic measures to reduce inventory and increase stock turnover.

This has been difficult to do in past years. Most vendors bully the smaller retailers into delivery dates and minimum quantities that don't work for the store. Many store owners have told me they were too afraid of not getting shipped or losing the vendor as a source of supply for certain items. Consequently they became submissive and resentful and had difficulty dealing with some of their vendors.

Such occurrences still happen, but the vendors are waking up in the '90s to some very rude awakenings. All along, the independent retailer has had to really fight to buy closer to the time of need, bucking what the bigger chains and specialty retailers were doing. Not so anymore. Fortunately for the independent, the big chains are also looking to "play it closer to the vest." Most chains are a lot larger than their vendors and can make these changes happen. The manufacturers in response are learning to work with their suppliers in a similar manner.

What does this all really mean? In the coming years, it will be not only necessary to buy smaller quantities closer to the time of need but this strategy will also be more common. Specialty chains and department stores are also using this strategy to stay more current with the customer's needs. Manufacturers will be producing merchandise close to the time of need. However, you will still have to fight and scrape with vendors over goods and for decent treatment.

Manufacturers who analyze their sales figures have discovered that small stores are the bulk of their business. They can't exist by selling only to the big guys. The big stores are having lots of problems, and manufacturers have to look to a diversified customer base to survive. This creates a more amenable, cooperative atmosphere for the buyer/vendor relationship to develop. Many reps have known this for years and fight for their customers on delivery and price with the manufacturer.

Keeping more current in your product mix will reduce your markdowns, adding to your gross margin. Watch the amount of markdowns in each department and subclass closely. Just as you look weekly at sales totals, the markdown totals clue you into downward trends. Cut off OTB for those areas and look for the new, upward trends.

Tally the sales for one week and project them out for the month (sales x 4 weeks for a ballpark monthly sales figure). Will you make your projections for the month? If not, look at what your upcoming promotions are for the month. Perhaps there is an event that will boost sales. One week of sales usually doesn't make for a trend, so it's not the time to panic—especially if you watch your sales and projected figures closely every week.

PROMOTE TO INCREASE SALES

Sales may just be lagging a bit, but to be safe rather than sorry, you decide to do some promotion in addition to what exists in your long-term marketing strategy. The quickest way to boost sales is to use your best categories. Yes, I said your best categories. We're not talking markdowns here.

You know what sells the best you see it every day. Offering special prices for a limited time on those items can push the purchasing decision into "now" instead of "later." This is the type of promoting that needs signs, which can be handled quickly.

Your sales records will prove that this type of promotion works. **Take time to think out what items you want to promote and what exactly the promotion will be.** Grouping or presenting a theme always helps.

1. Take a percentage off desired items or categories.

2. Offer another item free with a specific purchase.

3. Do a preferred customer sale or private sale, mailing out postcards to your mailing list. (Postcards can be printed quickly.)

I'm sure that you can see timing plays an important part in this strategy. This is a temporary markdown in specific areas or on specific products that make sense at the time. Out-of-season goods are more difficult to move at any price. Just picking any category and putting a sign in the window, in the mall, store or on the sidewalk won't do much good if the products and timing don't work together. Remember to give the customer value.

I have witnessed this approach work time and again when sales just weren't making plan. This should emphasize to you the wisdom of not placing purchases up to the full OTB amount for any one period of time.

Promoting like this can take advantage of your regular traffic. Keep that customer in mind as you select items or a category. Strong-selling items promoted with good signage do pick up sales.

REEVALUATING THE CURRENT OTB

There are many reasons sales rise and fall, including the weather, special events in your mall or across town, public construction (water department, gas, etc.), mall advertising or lack thereof, televised events (Super Bowl and such), political events (Desert Shield and Storm), even your neighboring store's promotional events. Whatever sales fluctuations you detect in your SPPR for the last month, you can see that some changes are needed in the projections of future months. After the second week of sales, you may already see that this has become necessary. (Multiply two weeks of sales by 2 for a view of the possible month's sales.)

Planning OTB and sales levels are your map; the results are the compass to your destination. Pull out all of your open order copies for the current month. Always review what is open. Goods that are selling well you want in the store. Stay on top of the vendor to ship you. Vendors that ship you late prevent you from controlling your inventory to the best of your ability. Take partial shipments only when necessary. Otherwise keep PO items together to control freight costs.

The current open orders will show you a variety of items and options for action:

1. **Get out of unwanted goods!** Unwanted goods are goods that are so close to being due that if they didn't ship two days ago you won't have them by the completion date. What to do?

Call the vendor to verify shipment. Get a weigh bill number. This proves that a carrier really did pick up the goods. (If the vendor was running late, they should have notified you offering you the opportunity to extend the completion date on your contract.) Items that appear marginal according to your sales trends should be canceled. Yes, canceled. I have had clients gasp at this idea and ask blankly, "Can you do that?" Yes. Your purchase order is a contract and the vendor is not holding up his or her part of it by not shipping on time.

This is a good reason to keep open order copies filed by completion date. It's easier than going through vendor files for the information. Keep on top of filing your open orders for a quick review of order status.

2. **Switch to strong-selling items!** Perhaps this vendor has another item that is selling well. Cancel the marginal items but substitute for them with the better-selling items. Do this if your selling trend supports taking in the merchandise.

3. **Change the delivery date!** Move the completion date to a later date. The order may contain goods that are new and fresh. You do want them, but would like to take them later. This is where you begin to develop your vendor/buyer relationship. A good rep will work with you in a give-and-take manner.

Vendors might say they can only ship to you when the goods are available. This may be a judgment call on your part. Manufacturers have been slow to learn that small retailers make up 80 percent of their business. I suggest working out delivery to develop a relationship. Very few goods hold a unique position. Drop vendors who obviously don't see the two-way street.

Several options exist between vendors and buyers. It takes some work creating a mutually beneficial relationship with your vendors. Feed them information. Take new items upon their suggestion. If they burn you, drop them from your supplier list. Good reps and vendors value the long-term relationship with a store. How else will they make money? You, too, will benefit from building for the long term with a vendor. When you need a favor, like canceling a style, you'll be taken care of cordially. The same goes when you need goods quickly or in larger quantity.

Evaluating your data allows you to better your turn and S/S Ratio. Depending on your trends, you either need to increase or decrease inventory. So far, we have looked at strategies to deal with the immediate problems. When you do this, also redo your OTB plan. This may include changing the planned S/S Ratio or basic stock level. You may need to change the sales projections, which obviously change the OTB. This is how you can truly control your inventory and make it perform to preserve and make profit.

Creating a give-and-take situation may mean placing new goods for a later time to replace what you canceled. If you are overbought or have lagging sales, the last thing you need is another order dropped on the floor by the UPS person.

OTHER CHANGES IN YOUR OTB PLAN

- You detect a major downturn in a subclass or department.
- A subclass or department is taking off.

Most of the previous tactics will work to change this around. Look to find the department taking up the slack, unless the store is in a downward trend. Another department may need more goods because it has taken off. Sometimes a subclass within a department has sales that carry the whole department. Look closely at this to see if it is time to make this a department on its own, with a stronger selection of goods. Then do projections for it with sales, S/S Ratio and OTB.

Take the steps to move out of the slower goods and change your original OTB plan to phase this department out. Obviously, this OTB for that department will no longer exist or at least have drastic changes.

Go back to the open orders again. Calculate what is open for future dates. How much did you place and is open? How much of it do you want and what can you get out of? If you have practiced ordering closer to the time of need, this should look pretty good. Otherwise, you will have to juggle your OTB dollars to reflect the sales trends.

To calculate actual dollars owned in inventory mid-month, remember to consider the amount of purchases you have received. When evaluating the OTB mid-month, look at:

- The total OTB for the month
- The dollar amount of purchases received to date for each department
- The balance of OTB available

The balance is the difference between the adjusted OTB and the purchases received to date. A quick, accurate way to figure OTB midstream looks like this:

Current Stock (BOM + purchases received)

+All On Order stock
– Projected Sales

= Balance of OTB for the month

Create a new OTB plan for the new department. Work with your vendors to find goods to build it up. Here is the tricky part. You don't want the total store figures to still show that you are overbought (or soon will be with current selling trends). Check your original listing of merchandising figures for the store to make sure that the total store position will be where you want it, with a safe level of inventory. Aggressiveness does pay off, but don't make the total store effort suffer from a narrow focus.

Evaluate the SPPR for each department and then look at the whole store. Every piece must come together. Always remember to visualize the total store and how any one component will work within it.

BETTERING YOUR FIGURES YEAR TO YEAR

The information in your SPPRs depicts on a grand scale where you came from, for each department and the total store. Side roads do exist that parallel and support it. One of these side roads supports your memory as much as the sales information collected in it. As mentioned earlier, there are reasons for how sales are and what they are.

Figures to Beat Book

Some call this a Daily Record, Sales Recap, or even The Book. Many retailers keep some kind of stenographer's pad or record book from a stationery store to record miscellaneous information that occurs daily.

Well, we are hardly talking about miscellaneous information! When you are up and running, you want to know as much as possible about what happened, or rather, how your sales occurred apart from the merchandising. Comparing a previous year's month to the upcoming year's month (March to March, April to April) you want to increase your store's sales over the previous year.

Let's say that you conducted an in-store promotion the third weekend of March coordinating with Easter (that year, Easter was at the end of March). You sent out 2,000 postcards, with 1,000 going to people on your mailing list and the other 1,000 going to names on a rented list that fit your customer profile.

Wow! You had a raging success on your hands, running out of all the wine, cheese and vegetable dips you ordered (we won't get into whether you planned this event well!), and your sales staff was run ragged taking care of the customers who responded. Now, how are you going to beat those figures?

Good question. I am glad you asked. This allows me to point out why you would write down your daily sales total in the "Daily Record" or "Figures to Beat" book. More than likely, neither you nor anyone else will remember everything about that event, except perhaps which Saturday it was held.

What you want to know on this side road:

- Last year's sales by day for the store
- What day of the week it was for each date
- What happened?

Now, you are asking me about the last point. Good question, again. Think this through:

- Did it rain, bringing people into your mall? Or drive them away from your strip center?
- Did the postcards get mailed on time? (Mailing too early or too late can hurt.)
- Did the mall give you an extra display space at the last minute?
- Did one of your salespeople call God and everyone else in their clientele book?

- What ads ran and in what media? Keep copies to keep improving your copy.

- What response did you get from the ad? Other than sales, what was the average sale with coupon? Which zip codes responded?

- Were two mailings or one dropped?

- Did the city come along and tear up the water main in front of your store and camp out for two weeks?

- Did you have a companion product giveaway on a Saturday? Was only store signage was used?

I could go on with this list; the factors affecting retail are many to say the least. If you want to beat last year's figures competently, first ask yourself if you can remember what happened every day of a month? It certainly does not reflect on your intelligence if you answer no. Your staff may have great memories. Trying to remember is a waste of time when you can quickly record the figures you already have together with daily occurrences as they happen.

Additional Benefits of a "Figures to Beat" Book

Salespeople also like to know ahead of time what goals you have set for them. If they at least can see the previous year's sales for that Saturday and the progress of each day for the month, you may see some highly motivated people. This can be especially true if you couple training and an open discussion of where you want the store to go.

All other planning, tracking and evaluating discussed previously related your data by total per month. You need to know more about how that month "happened" to evaluate trends and how you really will beat last year's figures. Any internal or external factors can contribute to that day's sales. Here are a few examples:

1. A specialty store next to a large department store in a mall simply couldn't do any business when that department store closed for inventory.

2. Street construction could all but kill an outdoor street location. The next year, if you're still open in some location, needs planning accordingly, without the hindrance of construction.

3. The weather can help some retailers, hinder others and it doesn't have to be bad weather. A nice day in an area where winter is pending could get people outside, but only in the parks, not shopping. Sudden cold weather ups coat and outerwear sales.

Again, thinking things like this through logically and from an objective viewpoint will serve you well. The upcoming information on interpreting consumer demand will add to this thought process and your ability to plan even further.

As you evaluate your merchandising figures to plan for the next year, this record will also assist you in plotting your marketing strategy. Whole books devoted to this subject are available in the library from fellow retailers or in bookstores. Some suggestions appear in the Bibliography (p. 123). As we move through this section, as in others, there are thoughts on marketing. Marketing is a part of merchandising for the retailer, but is in and of itself a subject needing scrutiny.

BOOSTING PROFIT MARGINS, BETTERING PRODUCT MIX

Testing Items

Gone are the days when all retailers have lived and died by the reorder. That used to be where you made your money for just about every type of store. Not any longer. Stores through the '80s became too much the same. However, an undercurrent began to emerge called the niche marketer. The focus for such a store is narrow and the selection deep. We have witnessed the development of stores that specialize in self-help books of every kind, everything a cat lover could possibly imagine and more, science toys, discount office supplies, car enthusiast related items and so on.

Testing items for reorder should not garner your focus going forward into the '90s, but instead, testing for trends. We have looked at this in our examples of setting up departments and subclasses. Reset your thinking to view category trends as opposed to items. Yes, there will be situations that substantiate keeping a basic stock and maintaining it with reorders. Watch this closely, as retail will continually evolve in the future. Watch for seasons that affect a basic area of inventory.

Examples:

Specialized Toy Store

Toys will come and go out of style, but certain types or specific items will be in demand at Christmas or another holiday every year (or so it will seem).

Bath/Linen and Related Products

Towels of a specific brand will always need to be in stock, but the colors will change continually according to trends. Sales may very well be slower at Christmas as a basic towel may not appear "gifty" to many consumers.

Specialty Foods

Mustards or some other sauce may become popular according to food trends, so you would look for brand selection and reorder carefully based on taste trends. Yes, there are food trends if you're one of those who is unconscious of them and simply woke up one day to realize that every restaurant had "blackened" something on their menu.

The above example points out, again, how trends in one area can affect another. Health consciousness trends affected a scope of service and product related fields. As you witness the beginnings of any trend, you can engineer testing of products to see how your customer will respond. If the response proves positive, you will seek other products to expand the inventory selection and satisfy this new desire. The evolution of trends will make this a continual process. Anyone who does not respond well to change should definitely stay out of retailing for a career. Of course, identifying trends is the source of the excitement as well!

Promotional Buying

From time to time, vendors will offer promotional merchandise. They aren't close-out items but goods made of materials they purchased at a discount or an assortment that has the costs averaged out to make the price per piece attractive to the retailer.

To evaluate such a purchase for your store, you need to look at the markon you will get, averaged out over a span of time and various selling prices. Usually the vendor quotes a minimum quantity along with the lower price. You will have to project out what you think is a feasible sell-through on the item(s). Your figures will look like this:

1st retail price x number of units

2nd retail price x number of units

3rd retail price x number of units

Add these totals together and figure the markon in relation to the total cost of the purchase.

$$\frac{\text{Total Selling Prices - Total Cost}}{\text{Total Selling Prices}} = \text{Average Markon}$$

INTERPRETING CONSUMER DEMAND

Consumers have needs and wants (perceived need to some), all affected by various economic, sociological and psychological factors. Consumers vary as these elements vary. The more trend-oriented your merchandise, the more these elements effect your business. This makes your job of watching the consumer's wants and needs a constant one, as you will be looking to interpret them.

Previously, I mentioned that you need to know your target market. You also want to know how to describe your customers by their motivations and how they select goods. Now, more than ever, the consumer will not be dictated to.

This store example illustrates this point. What is really shocking here is the buyer/owner's lack of logic in using what she already knew about her customer.

The store sells medium-priced women's apparel in a (very) Midwestern city. Short skirts had hit that level of manufacturers in a major way. (This does not mean that customers buy.) An article appeared in the newspaper describing how the customer had not "voted" for the shorter skirts and that the results really showed in lagging sales.

This buyer was quoted as saying (paraphrased), "Our customers are lower-middle to middle income working women who buy clothes to wear to work. We placed 40 percent of our skirt inventory in the shorter length and they just didn't move, even marked down."

Now I ask you, reading this book, and you who may be a first time retailer—if you had the above customer, would you put 40 percent of your skirt inventory for a season into short skirts? Of course not, because you would know that most Midwestern women then would never have worn a short skirt to the office. They might have worn one on the weekends, possibly, when being conservatively dressed would not be so important. Also, the income level could very well cause the purchase decision to be in "fun wear," garments that don't have to wear a long time and are usually priced slightly lower than clothes of more tailored nature.

I felt thoroughly embarrassed for this buyer/owner who was exposing such a faulty thought process in print for hundreds of thousands of people to read.

How do you know what the customer wants?
RESEARCH!

Which, for a small business, means reading your industry publications, marketing journals, financial newspapers and observing. Yes, observing. What do you see on the street? What are people talking about? What do your customers ask for? If people aren't asking for something, don't be lulled into feeling that everything is copasetic.

Segmenting the Market

Segmenting is dividing the whole market into a small homogeneous segment with similar characteristics. The characteristics you're looking for fall into four areas:

1. Demographic
2. Geographic
3. Psychographic
4. Behavioral

Demographic

These are population characteristics, including age, families, income, households, sex, occupation and education. This is a good isolation tool to identify a trend in the population, such as an increase in persons over 60. They have specific needs -thus an increase in that segment of the market means an increase in services and products for that segment. For example, empty-nester housing, medical in-home care and travel designed for their requirements.

You would usually use demographic statistics in conjunction with another segmenting base.

Geographic

This includes cities, counties, states, regions and type of region like rural or urban. Understand that populations are different from one area to another—state to state, suburban to urban, West Coast to Midwest, etc. Part of this difference also comes from the climate.

Psychographic

This refers to customer life style—one's living experiences, like work, social activities, leisure activities. Our interests, opinions and personality affect our life-style choices. Surveying your own customers (or potential customers in an area in which you're interested in locating) will give you the clues in this area. Ask about choices for leisure activities and opinions of ad sources, and have them answer with a degree of agreement from disagree to definitely agree with shades of agreement between.

Behavioral

Behavioral characteristics are found by grouping the consumers by their opinion of specific products or services, or their actual usage of them. Think of it as dollar votes, and the consumer may vote for a product with overwhelming support, mild support or no support (they're not buying it).

You can understand your market better through this type of segmentation in order to be able to identify the reasons for one group's usage or nonusage of a product/service.

Why Customers Buy

The buying motivation is why a product appeals to some customers and not to others, or why they "vote" for one product over another. The decision to vote is based on the complicated structure of each person. Wants and needs, emotional degrees of wants and needs, and functional aspects comprise the process that can be viewed from totally functional aspects to purely emotional satisfaction.

This section helps you start the thought process necessary to analyze your current customers or identify more fully a target market. Whether you are a start-up or are expanding and growing a current business, remember to be observant. Use the multitude of resources out there (mainly in your library) to better understand the consumer. Research is your watchword here!

The following is a list of buying motivations:

Quality	Color
Type of material	Ease of use
Brand name	Cost of care
Price	Status
Appropriateness	Convenience
Utility and functionality	

Your store data are excellent sources of information. You can analyze your data for indicators of these motivations. Also, ask your customers through surveys. If you have been trying to target new markets without having done any research, you may not have enough figures to show you a trend. Also, inconsistent product mix or hopping from one market to another will give you a poor indicator on what your customer is doing, since you probably haven't developed any identity in the eyes of the consumer.

These are the areas to look at for information on the buying motivations of your customers.

Markdowns

Want slips

Returns

Ad results

Surveys

Sales staff input

External Sources of Information

Competition

Resident buyers

Manufacturers and reps

Research studies and surveys (mostly done by associations)

Consumer and trade publications

Reporting services—Retail News Bureau

Consultants

Customer advisory groups
    (College boards, teen boards through high school or DECA
    [Distributive, Education Clubs of America], your own group)

Other Traits Your Store Can Tell You About

Additional information is at your fingertips, ready for inspection.

Know your customer intimately through the above information and by your average unit sale. The average is figured by dividing your dollar sales by the total number of transactions—by month, by season, whatever appears appropriate for your type of business. Don't make extra work for yourself for the sake of having statistics. However, figures can enlighten the retailer to the path of a better understanding of the customer and inventory, and to more profits. Some ECRs do this for you and you will simply have to record them. Knowing the amount of your sales in discounts given to your customers and employees can also help you.

The hourly report from your cash register tells you what time of day your customer wants to shop with you. A survey could also address this and could help determine what other hours they want, especially in the '90s given the ever-increasing two-income family.

ACTION LIST FOR CHAPTER 6

• Fill out a Sales and Purchase Performance Report each month.

• Look for sales and inventory trends, up and down, slow projected annual turns, low cumulative markon and excessive markdowns.

• Take action on inventories that are too high or too low for selling trend and projected sales.

• Adjust OTB in your plan accordingly.

• Set up a calendar or book for a "Figures to Beat" book. Write last year's sales for each day (Monday to Monday, etc.). Leave room to write down current situations, promotions, etc., for comparison next year.

Bibliography

The following books were used in my research for this book. I mention them here since some of them are quite good and you may want to take a look at them for your own library.

Burstinger, Irving. *Run Your Own Store—From Raising Money to Counting Profits* (Englewod Cliffs, NJ: Prentice Hall, 1989, 2nd edition)

Easterling, Cynthia. *Merchandising Mathematics for Retailing* (Englewood Cliffs, NJ: Prentice Hall, 1992).

Halloran, James. *The Entrepreneur's Guide to Starting a Successful Business* (Summit, PA: Liberty House, 1987)

Kamoroff, Bernard. *Small-Time Operator* (Laytonville, CA: Bell Springs Publishing, 1992)

Kneider, A.P. *Mathematics of Merchandising* (Summit, PA: Liberty House, 1987)

Levinson, Jay Conrad. *Guerrilla Marketing* (Houghton-Mifflin, 1984)

Phillips, Michael & Salli Rasberry. *Marketing Without Advertising* (Berkeley, CA: Nolo Press, 1986)

Stone, Elaine. *Fashion Buying* (New York: Gregg Division, McGraw Hill, 1989)

Wingate, Schaller & Bell. *Problems in Retail Merchandising* (Englewood CLiffs, NJ: Prentice Hall, 1973).

Other Resources

The following is a listing of books for the small business person published by Upstart Publishing Co., Inc. These publications on proven management techniques for small businesses are available from Upstart Publishing Co., Inc., 12 Portland St., Dover, NH 03820. For a free current catalog, call (800) 235-8866 outside New Hampshire, or 749-5071 in-state.

The Business Planning Guide, 6th edition, 1992, David H. Bangs, Jr. and Upstart Publishing Company, Inc. A manual that helps you write a business plan and financing proposal tailored to your business, your goals and your resources. Includes worksheets and checklists. (Softcover, 208 pp., $19.95)

The Market Planning Guide, 1990, David H. Bangs, Jr. and Upstart Publishing Company, Inc. A manual to help small-business owners put together a goal-oriented, resource-based marketing plan with action steps, benchmarks and time lines. Includes worksheets and checklists to make implementation and review easier. (Softcover, 160 pp., $19.95)

The Cash Flow Control Guide, 1990, David H. Bangs, Jr. and Upstart Publishing Company, Inc. A manual to help small-business owners solve their number one financial problem. Includes worksheets and checklists. (Softcover, 88 pp., $14.95)

The Personnel Planning Guide, 1988, David H. Bangs, Jr. and Upstart Publishing Company, Inc. A 176-page manual outlining practical, proven personnel management techniques, including hiring, managing, evaluating and compensating personnel. Includes worksheets and checklists. (Softcover, 176 pp., $19.95)

The Start Up Guide: A One-Year Plan for Entrepreneurs, 1989, David H. Bangs, Jr. and Upstart Publishing Company, Inc. This book utilizes the same step-by-step, no-jargon method as *The Business Planning Guide,* to help even those with no business training through the process of beginning a successful business. (Softcover, 160 pp., $19.95)

Managing By the Numbers: Financial Essentials for the Growing Business, 1992, David H. Bangs, Jr. and Upstart Publishing Company, Inc. Straightforward techniques for getting the maximum return with a minimum of detail in your business's financial management. (Softcover, 160 pp., $19.95)

Buy the Right Business—At the Right Price, 1990, Brian Knight and the Associates of Country Business, Inc., Upstart Publishing Company, Inc. Many people who would like to be in business for themselves think strictly of starting a business. In some cases, buying a going concern may be preferable—and just as affordable. (Softcover, 152 pp., $18.95)

Borrowing for Your Business, 1991, George M. Dawson, Upstart Publishing Company, Inc. This is a book for borrowers and about lenders. Includes detailed guidelines on how to select a bank and a banker, how to answer the lender's seven most important questions, how your banker looks at a loan and how to get a loan renewed. (Hardcover, 160 pp., $19.95)

The Home-Based Entrepreneur, 1993, Linda Pinson and Jerry Jinnett, Upstart Publishing Co., Inc. A step-by-step guide to all the issues surrounding starting a home-based business. Issues such as zoning, labor laws and licensing are discussed and forms are provided to get you on your way. (Softcover, 192 pp., $19.95)

Keeping the Books, 1993, Linda Pinson and Jerry Jinnett, Upstart Publishing Co., Inc. Basic business recordkeeping both explained and illustrated. Designed to give you a clear understanding of small business accounting by taking you step-by-step through general records, development of financial statements, tax reporting, scheduling and financial statement analysis. (Softcover, 208 pp., $19.95)

Target Marketing for the Small Business, 1993, Linda Pinson and Jerry Jinnett, Upstart Publishing Co., Inc. A comprehensive guide to marketing your business. This book not only shows you how to reach your customers, it also gives you a wealth of information on how to research that market through the use of library resources, questionnaires, demographics, etc. (Softcover, 176 pp.,$19.95)

On Your Own: A Woman's Guide to Starting Your Own Business, 2nd edition, 1993, Laurie Zuckerman, Upstart Publishing Company, Inc. *On Your Own* is for women who want hands-on, practical information about starting and running their own business. It deals honestly with issues like finding time for your business when you're also the primary care provider, societal biases against women and credit discrimination. (Softcover, 320 pp., $19.95)

Steps to Small Business Start-Up, 1993, Linda Pinson and Jerry Jinnett, Upstart Publishing Company, Inc. A step-by-step guide for starting and succeeding with a small or home-based business. Takes you through the mechanics of business start-up and gives an overview of information on such topics as copyrights, trademarks, legal structures, recordkeeping and marketing. (Softcover, 256 pp., $19.95)

Problem Employees, 1991, Dr. Peter Wylie and Dr. Mardy Grothe, Upstart Publishing Company, Inc. Provides managers and supervisors with a simple, practical and straightforward approach to help all employees, especially problem employees, significantly improve their work performance. (Softcover, 272 pp., $22.95)

The Woman Entrepreneur, 1992, Linda Pinson and Jerry Jinnett, Upstart Publishing Co, Inc. Thirty-three successful women business owners share their practical ideas for success and their sources for inspiration. (Softcover, 244 pp., $14.00)

Glossary

Accrual accounting: Accounting method that accounts for expenses and sales as they are incurred and invoiced. Calculates Cost of Goods Sold taking into account the beginning inventory (put into the cost) and the ending inventory (taken out of the cost).

Allowance from vendors: Any credits or cash discounts allowed by the vendor. This reduces your COGS.

Average markon: Markon averaged between several items being considered for purchase, usually for a promotion.

Beginning of the month (BOM): The inventory level in terms of retail dollars needed at the beginning of the month.

Cash basis accounting: Expenses are accounted for as they are paid out; the same for sales.

Classification and subclassification: Some stores break down the departments further than departments. Classifications are a more narrowly defined group under a department such as woven or knit under the women's top department. For small stores, it is best to use departments and subclasses with the subclasses for dresses being evening, prom, business, sleeveless summer and so on.

Chart of accounts: List of all items appearing on both balance sheet and Profit and Loss Statements.

Consignment purchases (as part of inventory): Goods not purchased outright by you. Some stores do this with new, small vendors to try them out. Remember, that this is inventory in your store and should not be disregarded in relation to your merchandise plan.

Cost of goods sold (COGS): The total cost of goods for any one-time period calculated by subtracting End of the Month Inventory from the Total Merchandise Handled and adding in the cost of freight, cleaning, repairing, etc. Any cash discounts would be subtracted from the sum to get a total figure for the COGS.

Credit terms: Those terms of payment allowed by the vendor stating discount rate (if any) with number of days to take discount and the amount of days total invoice is due.

Cumulative markon: The markon attained over a period of time. Just as in initial markon, this is the difference between total cost and total retail of all goods.

Deductions from other income: Any costs relating to the Other Income.

Department: The overall classification of similar types of goods, such as dresses, nonalcoholic beverages, linens, etc.

Deposit reconciliation: Financial control of daily deposits—a checks and balances—to maintain the bank drawer and balance sales against deposits. Hopefully sales and deposits always balance and you rarely have shortages (indicating problems in staff or accounting). A higher deposit is an overage.

Divisional merchandise manager: The person over the MMs (Merchandise Managers).

Electronic Cash Register (ECR): Not to be confused with POS (Point of Sale) terminals, which are computers. ECRs do have computer components and the ability to "talk" to computers but are not in themselves computers.

End of the month (EOM): The amount of inventory in terms of retail dollars left after sales and markdowns from the BOM.

Free on board (F.O.B.): In traffic language this term indicates at what point the buyer takes legal title to the goods and who is responsible for making claims against the carrier.

Gross margin: Most people don't distinguish this from Gross Profit, but please be advised that GM is the percent figure resulting from Gross Profit divided by the Net Sales. Gross Profit is the dollar figure.

Gross sales: All sales of the store(s) before any adjustments.

Maintained markon: Net Sales minus Gross COGS before any adjustments of cash discounts earned and alterations divided by Net Sales.

Markdowns: The dollar amount reducing the retail price of your inventory.

Markon: The percentage of the retail price on an item over and above cost. This figure is always in relationship to the retail price. In this light, the markon is the difference between retail and cost.

Merchandise manager: The person over the buyers for a department or departments in a large retail operation.

Net other income: The sum of the figures Other Income and Deductions from Other Income, found toward the end of the Income Statement before Net Profit.

Net profit: Profit amount after any additional income is added onto the Operating Profit and deductions relating to the Other Income are subtracted.

Net sales: The total sales of the store after employee discounts and returns.

Operating expenses: All those expenses that are incurred running your store.

Operating profit: The dollar amount and percentage of profit made from sales after deducting COGS and Operating Expenses.

Operating statement, P &L, Income Statement: The financial statement that depicts the profit overview encompassing operating expenses.

Open To Buy (OTB): The monthly dollar amount of inventory needed to bring inventory to the level planned for the next month.

Percentage increase <decrease>: The percentage increase <or decrease> of sales in a period of time, say a month, over the same period in the previous year. You will evaluate your departments and your total store increases and decreases.

Price Look Up (PLU): The number on an ECR. Price of item is programmed with the number to prevent ringing in of different prices on an item. Only the item number is keyed into the ECR.

Profit: What we all hope to make in our businesses. This is not so much a term here as a gentle reminder of one of the main reasons we are here doing this together.

Promotional allowance: An allowance specifically credited your store for promotions performed by you.

Purchases: The amount of goods purchased for resale in the store.

Returns and allowances: The dollar amount of goods returned to the store and any allowances made to customers in order to sell goods. This reduces the Gross Sales figure.

Returns to vendors: Goods returned to the vendor. This reduces the COGS in the period that it occurs

Safety levels: Planned levels of inventory for an item. This takes into account the lead time for the receipt of goods to prevent out-of-stock situations.

Sales per square foot: Annual sales figured on a square foot basis indicating productivity of inventory and the store itself. Total Net Sales are divided by the total square feet of the store to arrive at this annual benchmark figure.

Shrinkage: That amount of inventory that reduces your inventory figure due to a loss either on paper or the actual loss from the store.

Stock alterations: Any cost incurred to maintain or alter stock in order to make it saleable or to complete a sale.

Stock-to-sales ratio (S/S Ratio): The relationship between retail sales and the amount of inventory, planned or actual, at the beginning of the month at retail.

Stockturn: The number of times the average inventory totally turns through the store is sold and replaced, usually looked at annually.

Total merchandise handled: Beginning Inventory plus actual purchases. Most income statements do not show this figure.

Transfers: Goods moved out of one store into another. Goods transferred among stores prevent being overbought and taking excessive markdowns on goods that will sell better in one store over another.

Calculating Historical Figures for Existing Stores

Your goal here is to analyze what happened last year in inventory levels for each month in each department (if you have it separated out on your Profit and Loss Statements). Otherwise, you will only do a master plan for the total store with the historical inventory figures. Your other master OTB plans will show department sales figures with only the projected merchandising information.

OK, let's start attacking those numbers. Take your year end income statement (P & L) and get the total dollar sales figure and the total purchases figure (the Cost of Goods Sold). Use the gross margin percentage as a guide for the cumulative markon. To have a figure that will do you any good, use only the COGS figure without freight and discounts taken with the manufacturer. Figure the percentage of sales by dividing it by the Net Sales for the year. Now, pull out of your files the P &Ls for each month of the previous year.

The year end COGS percentage gives us the dividing factor that we need to find each month's inventory level. Use the master OTB format that is in the workbook to enter each month's figures that you calculate. This is what it will look like as you are doing your figures:

Let's say that the COGS figure for last year is 56 percent of net sales. You have in front of you the balance sheet for the previous January. Under assets, you find the inventory figure for the store (you can do this for every department that you track, if your accountant uses the type of program that prints out the accounting of beginning and ending inventory for each department you have set up on their system).

Now, divide it by the COGS percentage.

Example: January inventory on balance sheet is $32,692
Your COGS percentage for the year was 56%

$$\frac{\$32,692}{.56} = \$58,378.57$$

This figure indicates that the EOM for January was $58,378.57.

Not a very difficult thing to figure. It is much more difficult to describe how to do it. Now enter this figure on the line for "Last Year Inventory" under February. Continue to figure the other months until you have completed all twelve. Remember to look to the previous year's December inventory for the beginning inventory for January.

AN ALTERNATE METHOD

Some accountants leave the same inventory for every month on the balance sheet in between inventories taken. We will have to look at alternative past record evaluations in these cases. It will be only a ballpark figure. You may not have exact records of markdowns, but this will give you something to compare your current and future figures to.

Take the inventory figure of your last physical inventory and divide it by your COGS percentage as in the above formula. Chart your COGS percentage for the months following your inventory count.

Example:	Last Inventory	July	August	September
cost	$37,682	60%	56%	54.5%

The Retail Value of the physical inventory =

$$\frac{\$37,682}{.56} = \$67,289.28$$

What about the other month's inventory levels, you ask? Coming right up! There is a flow to your merchandise in the store since goods come in as purchases and go out as sales. Adding in the purchases to the inventory at a retail value and then subtracting out the sales figure will give you the next month's beginning inventory! This is the same as working on the OTB plan.

Example:

July purchases are $4,785

$4,785 ÷ .6 = $7,975

July BOM	$67,289.28
plus July purchases	7,975.00
	$75,264.28

July sales are $9,749

	$75,264.28
less July sales at retail	9,749.00
July EOM (or August BOM)	$65,515.28

Continue figuring the flow of goods to get the BOM for each month. Do this for a six-month planning period to see the validity of this comparison. This won't be exact, but the trend you will see can amaze you. Reviewing the dollars going through your store opens up whole new avenues to control your inventory and make your store more profitable.

The Chart of Accounts

ASSETS

CURRENT ASSETS

Cash

Deposits

Accounts Receivable

Inventory

Total Current Assets

FIXED ASSETS

Furniture, Fixtures & Equipment

Accumulative Depreciation, FF&E

Leasehold Improvements

Accumulative Depreciation, Lshld.

Total Fixed Assets

Total Assets

LIABILITIES & CAPITAL

CURRENT LIABILITIES

Trade Payables

Sales Tax Payable

Federal Income Tax Payable

State Income Tax Payable

Other Payroll Tax Payable

Total Current Liabilities

Long Term Liabilities

Loan, First Business Bank

Total Long Term Liabilities

CAPITAL

Owner's Draw*

Owner's Investment*

Previous Retained Earnings

Current Earnings

Total Capital

Total Capital and Liabilities

INCOME

SALES, Department 1

SALES, Department 2

SALES, Department 3

SALES, Department 4

SALES, Department 5

Returns & Allowances

Net Sales

COST OF GOODS SOLD

PURCHASES, Department 1

PURCHASES, Department 2

PURCHASES, Department 3

PURCHASES, Department 4

PURCHASES, Department 5

Cash Discounts & Allowances

Total Cost of Goods Sold

GROSS PROFIT

OPERATING EXPENSES

Salaries

Payroll Taxes

Commissions

Rent

Utilities

Telephone

Long Distance Telephone

Business Insurance

Health Insurance

Selling Supplies

Office Supplies

Postage

Advertising

Printing

Professional Fees

Dues & Subscriptions

Repair & Maintenance

Licenses & Misc. Taxes

Educational

Donations

Travel Expenses

Entertainment

Miscellaneous

    Total Expenses

OTHER INCOME

OTHER EXPENSES

NET INCOME BEFORE TAXES

INCOME TAXES

*Note: A corporation will not have owner's draw or owner's investment. Instead, the capital section will show owner's equity and other stock distribution by monies paid for the stock being the investment. Check with your accountant for proper calculation and recording of equity.

Blank Forms

The following blank forms are for you to fill out and use.

DAILY TALLY SHEET

Department_____ Subclass_____

Week/Month_____

Date	Code#	Vendor	Description	Price	Tally	Qty.	Total Dollars
							Totals:
							_____

DAILY TALLY SHEET

Week of:_____

Date	Dept/ Sub#	Vndr #	Item Description	Price Sold	Hash (Tally)	Count Sold	Qty. Dollars	Total

Week Total:_____

PURCHASE ORDER

DATE:_____   P.O.#_____

TO:_____   SHIP/BILL _____

_____   _____

_____   _____

_____   _____

SHIPPING INSTRUCTIONS

Terms:_____   Carrier:_____

                                              Start Ship Date:_____

F.O.B.   To Arrive:_____

                                              Cancel Date: _____

Misc. Instructions:

_____

_____

_____

#	Description	Qty.	Unit	Cost	Tot.$	Retail	R. Tot	D/Sub

TOTALS: _____   _____   _____

Order number must appear on all invoices.

                    BUYER:_____

All changes in order must by cleared with person of above signature either by telephone or in writing. We reserve the right to refuse goods that arrive after the cancel date.

OPEN ORDER RECORD

DEPARTMENT_____ MONTH_____

P.O. #	Vender Name	Ship Date	Comp Date	Stock # and Description	#of PCS	Cost EA.	RTL. EA.	TOT. Cost	TOT. RTL.

TOTALS _____

PRICE CHANGES — MARKDOWNS & MARKONS

Markdown:_____ Temporary?_____ Permanent?_____ Department_____

Markon:_____ Date

• Taken:_____

Name/# Vendor	Hash Count	Code # /Sub.	Product Description	Orig Rtl.	Mrkdwn $	Mrkup $e	Diff +/-	Total Diff.	Comment

TOTAL_____

PURCHASES RECEIVED AND RETURNS TO VENDOR RECORD

DEPARTMENT_____SUBCLASS_____ MONTH____

P.O. #	VENDR NAME	DATE RECD.	COMP DATE	STOCK # AND DESCRIPTION	#OF PCS	COST EA.	RTL. EA.	TOT. COST	TOT. RTL.

TOTALS_____

RETURN TO VENDOR RECORD

INVC.#	VNDR.	REC'D	AUTH#	ITEM# & DESCRIP.	QTY.	COST	RTL.	T.CST	T.RTL

DAILY DEPOSIT RECONCILIATION AND SALES RECORD

SALES from register readings

    Cash and Checks   _____

    Mastercard/Visa   _____

    American Express   _____

    Gross Sales   _____

    Discounts and Returns   _____

    Adjusted Gross Sales   _____

Breakdown of sales per register readings

    Net Sales   _____

    Gift Certificates Sold   _____

    Gift Cert. Redeemed   _____

    Shipping Fees   _____

    Total Merchandise Sales   _____

    (This is merchandise sold, not all monies taken into the store.)

    Record Sales and Non-Taxable Merchandise Sales
    for sales tax reporting: _____

    Non-Taxable Sales   _____

    Taxable Sales   _____

DEPOSIT Calculation

    CASH   +_____

    CHECKS   +_____

    MC/VISA   +_____

    AM.EX.   +_____

    TOTAL DEPOSIT   =_____

TO BALANCE Deposit:

    Adjusted Gross Sales

    + Gift Certificates Sold

    - Gift Cert. Redeemed

    - Petty Cash

    _____

    = Deposit Amount   _____
    (Deposit amount should match
    TOTAL DEPOSIT figure above.)

OVER/<UNDER>   _____

PETTY CASH PAID OUT (description of transactions paid):

SALES AND PURCHASE PERFORMANCE REPORT

DEPARTMENT/TOTAL STORE

Prev. EOM	MONTH/			MONTH/			MONTH/		
	L.Y	Plan	Actual	L.Y	Plan	Actual	L.Y.	Plan	Actual

S/S Ratio									
Sales									
% Inc.<Dec>									
Plan MDs									
Revised Plan									
BOM (@ Retail)									
Revised Plan									
On Order									
Open To Buy									
Purc.Recd.									
MDs taken									
Revised OTB									

Recap for Period   Remarks

	Cost	Retail	avg.initial markon %	avg. stock
1. Net purchases				
2. Stock on Hand @ beg of period				
3. Total Mdse Handled				annual turn
4. Net Sales				
5. Markdowns				
6. Markons		Dept:_____		
7. Out of Stocks		%of total		store total
8. Shrinkage		Mo.1		
9. Total adjustments		Mo.2		
10. Ending Inv. @ end of period		Mo.3		

PERPETUAL INVENTORY SHEET

DEPARTMENT_____   SUBCLASS_____   MONTH_____

Stock #	Description & Vendor Name	Vndr Stk#	RTL $	CST $	BOM	WK 1	WK 2	WK 3	WK 4	WK 5	TOT $	EOM	OO

MONTH TOTALS_____

OPEN TO BUY

Department _____ Year _____

MONTH	Month	Month	Month	Month	Month	Month	Month	Month	Month	Month	Month	TOTAL	Month
Projected Sales													
Projected S/S Ratio													
Beginning Inventory													
Markdowns													
OPEN-TO-BUY													
Last Year's Sales													
Last Year's Inventory													
Last Year's S/S Ratio													
EOM													

Notes from last year

Notes re: department increases and decreases

Notes on changing S/S Ratio

Projected Stockturn _____

Proj. Average S/S Ratio _____

Proj. Average Stock _____

Proj. Average Sales _____

SIX-MONTH CASH FLOW PROJECTIONS

	Mo.___	Mo.___	Mo.___	Mo.___	Mo.___	Mo.___	Totals
Cash On Hand							
Sales/Receipts							
Collections							
Loans/Other Injections							
Total Cash Receipts							
Total Cash on Hand							
Operating Expenses							
Purchases/Inventory							
Salaries							
Payroll Taxes							
Advertising							
Bad Checks/Debts							
Subscriptions/Assoc.							
Professional Fees							
Freight Out							
Office and Postage							
Rent and Common Area							
Utilities and Telephone							
Insurance							
Taxes and Licenses							
Supplies							
S.C. on Credit Cards							
Bank Charges							
Miscellaneous							
Interest on Loan							
Subtotal/Expenses							
Loan Principle Payment							
Capital Purchases							
Other Start-Ups							
Owner's Draw							
Total Cash Paid Out							
Ending Cash							

Index

Computerizing Your Inventory System

When do you need to put your system on a computer?

1. You see too many mistakes in the recordkeeping.
2. You can't seem to keep up with it.
3. You feel like there must be some valuable information you're not getting or your information is not as accurate as it could be.
4. Your business is showing healthy increases, better than your competitors and/or over national averages.

Any store doing over $200,000 needs to look at collecting data on a computerized system. Once your store grows to the point that you can see staying on a manual system will hurt your business, it's time to automate.

Low-cost systems didn't exist before now. Most systems currently available are expensive or weren't written by retailers.

Retail Strategies and Publishing, Inc., originally published this book as a result of the needs of clients. Software was a natural next step. Our software is for retailers by retailers experienced in independent, small-store operations.

Benefits of capturing your data on a computer:

- You the buyer/owner have more time with customers and can make the best selections possible for the customer.
- Data is captured faster.
- Calculations are performed automatically.

Partial listing of reports from RS&Ps management software:

- Vendor analysis with purchases, markdowns, returns, average unit pricing and profitability.
- Purchase order generation in the program —no open order forms to fill out—tracks partially received orders as well
- Current on order figures by vendor and department
- Available OTB
- Weekly and monthly sales figures compared to previous years.

The program offers easy view and entry with pop-up windows for specific entry and general help. Includes automatic markon calculation from the markons you set up in your system. Eliminate the pencil and eraser.

Use the Form Below (or a Photocopy) to Request More Information on the Computer Program

NAME_____

ADDRESS_____

ADD. 2 _____

CITY _____STATE_____ZIP_____

I copied this from a library book

My store has been open for_____years.

I am opening a store in the next _____year(s), _____months.